THE ART OF GROWING OLD

By

Bertrand Stephen St. Louis

GULF BOOK
SERVICES

All rights reserved. No part of this publication may be reproduced, stored in a retrieval system, or transmitted in any form or by any means, electronic, mechanical, photocopying, recording or otherwise, except for the use of quotations in book reviews, without the prior permission of the author.

Copyright © Bertrand Stephen St. Louis 2024

The views and opinions expressed in the book are the author's own and the facts as reported by him have been verified to the extent possible, and the publisher is not in any way liable for the same.

GULF BOOK SERVICES

Published by Gulf Book Services Ltd
20-22 Wenlock Road, London, NI 7GU, UK
Email: info@gulfbooks.co.uk

Office No: G23, Sharjah Publishing City Freezone, Sharjah – UAE

First Published in Gulf Book Services Ltd
First paperback edition October 2024

Co-Author – Timothy St. Louis
Cover Concept – Mohamed Reshad
Writing Consultant - Nisha Sanjeev
Book Design – Madhavi S
ISBN 978-1-917529-00-6 (paperback)

Typeset in Times Roman and Lumios Marker by
Forging Minds, India

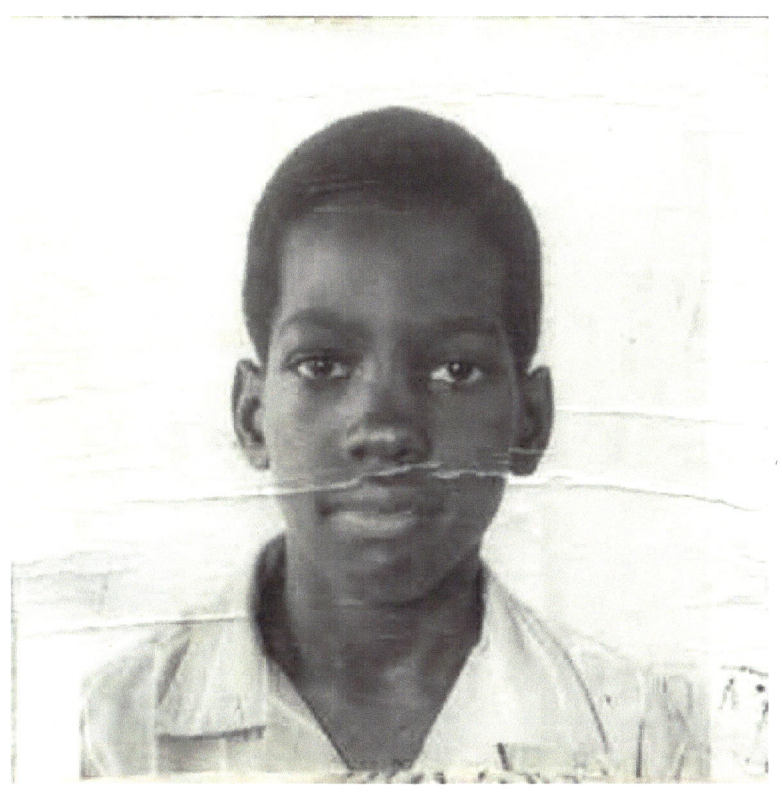

DEDICATION

I dedicate this book to myself, Bertrand Stephen St. Louis

To the past me:

You have fulfilled your dreams and have accomplished so much. You have the love of your family and the respect of your peers and the world. Great job! You have given immensely and now is the time to unapologetically give back to yourself.

To the present me:

Live and enjoy the present. Live with intention. This is what matters now.

To the future me:

There is no stopping now. Age does not mean the end. Continue to strive to be and feel your best so you can complete your future goals and keep experiencing more firsts.

I alone have the power to make myself happy!

Whatever is placed at my feet may influence my decision to be happy, yet it's up to me. No one has the power nor the control over another human to make them happy. Not even God uses that power.

All we can do is 'give back' whatever we decide to place at their feet. Then, they themselves will decide or choose to use what they are given, all through life, to make themselves happy.

Each of us is responsible for our own happiness.

I am giving back to myself!

I choose me!

CONTENTS

Foreword   xiii

Introduction   xv

SECTION: I- Ageless truths

Truth #1: Old age is not a number	3
Truth #2: Old age is not retirement time	7
Truth #3: Old age is not rainy day	13
Truth #4: Old people smell	17

SECTION: II - Alone not lonely

Why I wanted to touch my toes	37
How to deal with frustrated family	41
How to deal with loss of friends	51
It's a life-time partnership	57
Setting stage for the final act	63
Purpose, passion & personal priority	69

SECTION: III - Rekindling passion

A Trinidadian's green thumb	85
I'm a star playing house at 60	89
Be a new you	95
I'm no Rapunzel in the digital era	101
The write act beyond retirement	109
Become an entrepreneur	117
Earn in your PJs	125
Become a silver influencer	133
Start an NGO	143
Be creative	151

SECTION: IV - Growing old the Gen X, Millennial & Gen Z way

Growing old is having lived a life on your own terms	173
10 timeless truths I wish for the young	185
From an idealistic view at 22 to reality at 62	193
My end-of-life strategy… applaud myself	201
10 tips to nurture connection across generations	207

SECTION: V - Silver seniors

Sandi Rich Saksena rocking at 72	227
Ahmad Al Awadhi Rukni is an art ambassador at 65	235
Anjini Laitu aims to be world's top abstract painter at 83	243
The math of aging stops at giving back to self	251

The Art of Growing Old

FOREWORD

In the journey of life, there are pivotal figures who shape our paths, and for me, that guiding light has been my father. You may know him as Mr. B, but I know him as Bertrand St. Louis. From the tender age of four, when I received my first upright piano, to the unexpected adventures like our spontaneous trip to Tijuana, Mexico, for my 18th birthday, my father has infused my life with love, wisdom, and boundless opportunities.

Reflecting on my upbringing, I realize how fortunate I've been to have experienced unwavering support and guidance. Not every child is blessed with such a nurturing environment, and for that, I am eternally grateful.

As I matured into adulthood, I witnessed my father's commitment to self-care and personal growth, which inspired me to embark on my own journey of self-discovery. Through his example, I learned the true essence of greatness - not merely in achievements but in the relentless pursuit of excellence and self-awareness.

The Art of Growing Old

Now, as I stand on the threshold of my own legacy, I am humbled to carry forward the values instilled in me by my father. This book, *The Art of Growing Old*, symbolizes more than just words on paper; it represents a convergence of past, present, and future - a testament to the enduring power of familial love and the pursuit of greatness.

Within these pages, you'll find not only a roadmap to personal fulfillment but also a celebration of the human spirit as it navigates the complexities of aging. *The Art of Growing Old* invites you to explore the richness of life's experiences, to embrace the passage of time with grace and dignity, and to discover the beauty in every stage of life.

It is my sincerest hope that you'll embark on this journey with an open heart and a willingness to explore the depths of your own potential. May this book serve as a beacon of inspiration for generations to come, guiding us all toward a greater understanding of what it means to grow old with wisdom, grace, and purpose.

- Indy Nyles aka TDS St. Louis

INTRODUCTION
From 18's illusion to 60's wisdom

As a young boy, I eagerly awaited to grow up to experience the freedom and independence it promised. The age of eighteen was considered a standard milestone in the Americas, granting the privilege of obtaining a driver's license to operate a motor vehicle.

At the age of eighteen, the expectations were high—I was supposed to complete high school and potentially move on to college, learn a trade, or join the military. Additionally, this age made me eligible for marriage and starting a family, marking a significant point where I could take full responsibility for my actions in the eyes of God and man.

With the advent of eighteen came a plethora of options, both positive and negative, and I looked forward to reaching this pivotal point in my life. However, when the fateful day arrived in 1980, my eighteenth birthday came
and went without any fanfare. I found myself at a loss, not truly understanding where I stood in the timeline of my life and uncertain about what lay ahead.

The Art of Growing Old

On June 12th, 1980, I experienced the milestone of graduation, and by June 24th, 1980, I followed my mother's advice and ventured to California with the expectation of attending school, securing a job, starting a family, and embracing a happily-ever-after scenario.

Fast forward forty-four years later and I find myself not in California post the routine job-life, instead I am grappling with the swift passage of time and feeling a sense of age creeping in. Now I ponder what transpired, how I arrived at this point, the seemingly rapid pace of life, and whether this feeling of age is indeed the onset of old age.

Back then, at eighteen, what I knew was the prologue,
A mere introduction to life's grand dialogue.
Now, the climax unfolds, the actual tale,
At sixty-three, life's symphony, I fully scale.
I am happy you are holding this book
Where youth's notions of old age I'll unhook;
Decades have shown the myths that didn't stay,
The true meaning of aging, I'll convey.

I promise to share what it means to truly grow old,
How I feel about it, and personal stories I'll unfold;

The Art of Growing Old

I take pride in the journey that I've embraced,
Maturing, thriving, with life interlaced;
So, let's cease the battle, this age-old fight,

Embrace it instead, with all of our might.
In this book, my wisdom, lived through and true,
A guide to aging gracefully, just for you.

Bertrand Stephen St. Louis

The Art of Growing Old

SECTION: I
Ageless Truths

Wrinkles are roadmaps not expiration dates

The Art of Growing Old

Truth #1:
Old age is not a number

The numbers are adding up and it's being felt day by day. Then why does it seem that it's going so fast? Why does it feel like the clock is racing ahead? As if the hands of the clock have conspired to outpace our yearnings, pushing us further into the future against our will.

As we juggle the demands of life, the very essence of time seems elusive, slipping through our fingers as we strive to grasp onto moments that seem to dissolve into the past.

One thought I often reflect on is the percentage of time each passing day, week, or month represents in the overall span of our lives. The paradox unfolds as the longer we live, each passing year signifies a diminishing percentage of the total years we've lived.

The Art of Growing Old

Our first year represents 100 percent of our life. In year 10, one year represents 10 percent of our life lived, and so on. Each annual journey accounts for a mere 10 percent of our life's narrative. Imagine the shrinkage of percentage as we reach the milestone of 50 years – by then, each passing year constitutes a mere 2 percent of our storied existence.

This exponential shrinkage in significance might be the elusive culprit behind the illusion that time accelerates with each passing year. Yet, amidst this perceived hastening, we acknowledge the unchanging rhythm of 60 seconds in a minute, 60 minutes in an hour, and the completion of 365 days in a year. Day by day, we chug along, calling it one day at a time and fulfilling a sense of purpose as we age.

While the numbers themselves may not deceive, we often claim that age is just a number. The nuance lies not merely in counting the years but in infusing each numeral with purpose and meaning. It's about making the numbers count, not just acknowledging its existence—a distinction that adds depth to the evolving narrative of our lives.

As a young boy, even I had bought into the popular narrative believing that I would eternally bask in the vitality of youth, be perpetually vigorous, able to seize every opportunity without constraint.

Today, the invincibility of my earlier years has gracefully surrendered to the acknowledgment of my own mortality.

In navigating this reality, I've come to appreciate that while age is, indeed, just a number, it is also a repository of memories, a measure of resilience, and a testament to the ceaseless evolution of myself. Even now the freedom to do as I please persists, however, it is richer, shaded with the hues of my humongous experience and a deeper understanding of the choices that I want to define my journey.

The Art of Growing Old

Truth #2: Old age is not retirement time

Most Baby Boomers and Gen X believe in retirement age. I never subscribed to this. Can you retire, as in absolutely retire and do nothing, after a particular age? Is that practical an idea? Perhaps for the ultra-wealthy. It's often not practical for many middle-class individuals due to financial, healthcare, and lifestyle considerations.

Retirement represents a departure from the structured routines and professional demands that characterized earlier years. It's a period when individuals, having contributed significantly to their careers and communities, now have the opportunity to explore a different dimension of life. The liabilities, responsibilities and demands have, no doubt, eased. Beyond the conventional notions of slowing down, it is an era that beckons individuals to redefine purpose, explore passions, and savor the richness of each passing moment. And that requires financial and moral support.

A reason some individuals choose not to retire in the traditional sense, opting for continued engagement in meaningful work or pursuing entrepreneurial ventures. When retired, there is an endless stream of concerns about being or becoming old - from financial security to personal well-being and healthy living.

Let's look at some common concerns the middle-class retirees face.

Financial Considerations:

Have you figured in inflation? Middle-class individuals often rely on savings and investments, such as retirement accounts and social security, to sustain their lifestyle in retirement. These may not provide sufficient funds to retire comfortably without any income.

The cost of living tends to rise over time due to inflation. Without a source of income, retirees may struggle to keep up with increasing expenses, such as healthcare and housing.

Longevity and Healthcare:

Thanks to medical breakthroughs, people are living longer, and retirement could potentially last for several decades. This makes it challenging to save enough to support a long retirement without some form of income. Medical expenses tend to increase with age, making it necessary to have funds set aside for health-related costs.

Lifestyle Choices:

Lifestyle is something most cannot compromise on. Many people want to maintain a certain standard of living in retirement, which might require ongoing income to cover expenses like travel, hobbies, or dining out.

Unforeseen Expenses:

No one can foresee emergencies – personal or family. Even if you were to ignore that, what about unexpected expenses such as home repairs, vehicle maintenance, natural disasters, or legal issues. Having a source of income can help cope with these situations.

Psychological Considerations:

Work life often provides people with a sense of purpose, social interaction, and mental stimulation. Complete retirement may lead to boredom, social isolation and lack of fulfillment for some people. This can lead to psychological concerns.

Changing Goals:

This is common among seniors. Some individuals take up new interests or begin to nurture old passions, now that they have time to themselves. So, what about financial resources? Pursuing these goals might necessitate additional income.

Social Security and Debt:

Social security benefits alone may not be sufficient to cover all living expenses. Pensions are becoming less common, and many retirees rely on personal savings. Middle-class individuals may carry mortgages, student loans, or other debts into retirement.

Economic Uncertainty:

Economic downturns can significantly impact investments and savings, affecting one's ability to retire comfortably. Relying solely on investments to fund retirement can be risky, as the stock market can be volatile.

Legacy:

Some retirees take pride in leaving an inheritance for their children. Some want to support charitable causes, which may require ongoing financial planning.

All the above boils down to being financially wise.

The Art of Growing Old

Truth #3: Old age is not rainy day

It is normal to be concerned about financial security throughout our adult lives. As we get older, the concern is considered front and center. In fact, we are often reminded to prepare for financial security in our younger years, so that it does not become a problem in retirement years or when we are older. Some even say prepare for that rainy day, but I do not view retirement or aging as a rainy day.

Rainy days to me are more of the preparation for an emergency. I have always had a practical approach to life. Perhaps having a humble childhood, I knew the importance of being prepared at all times – be that financially, mentally and emotionally. Sometimes we hear that we must have a three-month stash for the unforeseen. Many of us live paycheck to paycheck making it difficult to have excess to accumulate that three months' fund. However, those of us that are able to, should consider going further with the aim of collecting a six-month emergency stash.

Although many may not be able to value this amount in cash, there are reasons more so than not to start collecting six months' worth of rice and beans, along with non-perishable staples, in the event of supply interruptions or other emergencies.

Pundits often lay out strategies for saving during our working years, either to generate investments in their companies or to give good advice. Other advisors give financial guidance with an eye towards getting old. Often times I see them speaking from a high-level or a level that represents what I call the upper echelon of society or the more wishful thinking of society.

This could be because myself and maybe many others are not able to attain the stated goal or the recommended goals they lay out or portray to us. Nevertheless, we can benefit from what's being said because we still need to be in some state of financial security, or financial stability as we get older.

We still need a source of revenue to get us through our senior years.

In the United States, most seniors look forward to the government social system called 'social security'. Social security is like an insurance fund that's paid in throughout all of our working years with payouts calculated using the number of working years and the annual income each year. So when you retire or become disabled, you, your spouse, and your dependent children, if any, can receive monthly benefits that are based on your life-long reported earnings. Many times, these amounts are insufficient to cover the needed expenses during the senior years so an additional source of income will be needed.

Depending on the type of income generated during junior years, coupled with the annual expenses for supporting self and family, many will live paycheck to paycheck. Yet, with some planning and a little sacrifice during junior years, we can save or invest a little to supplement the social security value.

Many juniors put off certain financially impacted activities for when they become seniors, with the notion that it may cost less later in life than sooner.

It could be true that many expenses are higher during our junior years than our senior years, yet there are factors that come into play during the senior years that can impact our financial stability, notably, such as our health.

Truth #4:
Old people smell

Physical, mental, and emotional health are interconnected. Neglecting one aspect can have a cascading effect on the others, especially as we grow older. For instance, an older person who suffers from arthritis may experience frustration and sadness due to decreased mobility. This can negatively impact their mental and emotional well-being.

Given that mental health is closely linked to cognitive function and memory, a subsequent cognitive decline, such as dementia or Alzheimer's, can significantly affect emotional well-being. An individual experiencing depression may have difficulty concentrating and remembering important information, affecting their daily life and overall emotional health.

As emotional health plays a pivotal role in social interactions, feelings of loneliness and social isolation can exacerbate conditions like depression and anxiety and can even impact one's immune system.

We spoke of financial security in the earlier pages; this is a major stress inducing factor. Emotional health is linked to the body's stress response, too. An older adult who constantly worries about financial issues may experience chronic stress, which can lead to hypertension and other cardiovascular problems.

Therefore, mental and emotional health significantly influence lifestyle choices. An elderly individual who is content and emotionally balanced may be more motivated to maintain an active lifestyle, making it easier for them to stay physically healthy. I have always prioritized my mental and emotional well-being.

One thing I noticed among my peers is that they perceive grooming as less important even when they are careful about their health. Grooming is not their palette. Grooming is much more than mere aesthetics; it has a profound impact on self-esteem, social interactions, health, and overall quality of life. Continuing to care for one's appearance and hygiene can significantly contribute to a positive outlook and overall well-being.

Consider these…

Self-Esteem and Confidence:

Grooming plays a significant role in how people perceive themselves. When someone takes the time to groom, it often leads to a sense of well-being and improved self-esteem. Feeling good about one's appearance can positively affect confidence, which is essential for maintaining a positive outlook and mental health.

Social Interactions:

Personal grooming is closely linked to social interactions. It can impact how others perceive and respond to you. Maintaining a well-groomed appearance can help foster positive social relationships and interactions, which are vital for mental and emotional well-being. People are often more comfortable and confident when they know they look their best.

Health and Hygiene:

Basic everyday grooming, such as regular bathing, dental

care, and hair care, can help prevent various health issues. These practices can boost self-care, which is integral to both physical and emotional health.

Sense of Normalcy:

Continuing grooming routines provides a sense of normalcy and structure in daily life. It can serve as a form of self-discipline, which can be particularly important in later stages of life when routines become even more essential for overall well-being.

Sense of Dignity:

Maintaining personal hygiene and grooming even as one ages can contribute to a sense of dignity. Feeling clean and well-groomed helps individuals maintain a positive self-image and sense of worth, which is vital for emotional health.

Mental Health:

Grooming can be a therapeutic and meditative practice. The act of caring for oneself can have a calming and stress-relieving effect. It provides an opportunity to focus on self-care and mindfulness, which can improve mental health.

Adaptation to Change:

As people age, they may face changes in their appearance, such as graying hair or wrinkles. Proper grooming allows individuals to adapt to these changes gracefully and confidently, which can positively affect their self-perception and emotional well-being.

The way I look makes me feel dignified, so I always try to dress the part. If I feel down any given day, I will dress up even more and this is important to me so as to lift myself up.

Have you heard of 'old people smell'? I had a discussion with a colleague about this. We disputed as to whether or not there was such a thing. The question that arose was whether or not there was a scientific explanation for the idea of 'old people smell'. My research suggests there is.

According to the insights shared in a blog post on Franklin Park's website, as our skin matures, its inherent antioxidant protection diminishes. This reduction in natural defenses leads to increased oxidation of lipid acid. Consequently, the oxidation process produces a chemical compound known as nonenal, which is responsible for emitting the distinct 'old people smell' that many of us recognize.

The Art of Growing Old

This leads me to a subject I am deeply passionate about: hygiene as we age. Recognizing that certain aspects of the aging process are beyond our control; the aging journey introduces scientific changes that necessitate corresponding physical adjustments.

From dental care and grooming routines to the duration I wear my clothes and the length to which I maintain my hair, every detail holds significance for me. These factors have a direct impact on my mental health, as I am mindful of the potential influence on others. While I'm not suggesting that my aging process will repulse others, it serves as a constant reminder to be aware of these needs.

My appearance is crucial because our self-perception significantly influences our emotional well-being. Regular showers, ranging from once a day to multiple times a day, contribute to a sense of freshness and comfort.
As Bruce Springsteen's lyrics in *I'm on Fire* convey, waking up with sheets soaked in sweat becomes more common as we age. Thus, regular laundering of bedding becomes essential. While not everyone may have the means to wash frequently, maintaining cleanliness in our clothing contributes to dignified aging. If resource conservation is a

concern, other priorities can be considered, but compromising on hygiene is not advisable.

Another critical area, speaking of priorities, is our dietary choices. What and how much we eat, as well as the timing of our meals, can significantly impact our health. In the United States and globally, many seniors face substantial health-related costs, including those associated with health insurance and prescription drugs.

Medical service providers and pharmaceutical companies may adopt a 'pay me now or pay me later' approach. Addressing these concepts through our food choices seems a proactive strategy. Opting for a nutritious diet can be likened to investing in our health insurance, potentially reducing long-term costs.

Without delving into exhaustive details, the essence is that we should strive to afford and consume the best quality food available to contribute to our long-term health and happiness. Ultimately, the overarching goal is to do what we can do to our utmost best, without becoming a liability to family, friends, and society throughout the remainder of our lives.

MINDFUL MUSINGS

How do you perceive the concept of age? Do you agree that old age is not defined by a number? Why or why not?

_____

_____

_____

_____

Reflect on a time when you felt much younger or older than your actual age. What factors contributed to that feeling?

_____

_____

_____

_____

_____

What are your thoughts on retirement? Do you see it as a time to stop working or a chance to pursue new interests?

_____

_____

_____

_____

Describe your ideal definition of retirement. What activities or passions would you like to explore?

_____

_____

_____

_____

_____

How do you view aging in terms of positivity and opportunities? Do you see it as a time for decline or growth?

_____

_____

_____

_____

_____

Write about an older person you admire. What qualities or achievements make their life inspiring to you?

_____

___

___

___

___

What stereotypes about aging do you hold or have encountered? How do these stereotypes affect your perception of old age?

___

___

___

___

___

Reflect on the phrase 'old people smell'. How do societal attitudes and prejudices about aging influence our views and interactions with older individuals?

_____

_____

_____

_____

How do you feel about your own aging process? Are there any fears or concerns you have about getting older?

_____

_____

_____

_____

What steps can you take to ensure that your later years are fulfilling and enjoyable?

_____

_____

_____

_____

How do you define a meaningful life beyond your professional career? What hobbies, interests, or causes are you passionate about?

_____

_____

_____

_____

The Art of Growing Old

_____

What legacy do you wish to leave behind, and how can you start building it now?

_____

_____

_____

_____

Have you ever felt judged or stereotyped based on your age? How did that experience affect you?

_____

_____

_____

_____

_____

What can you do to challenge and break down age-related stereotypes in your community?

_____

_____

_____

_____

How do you envision your future self? What steps can you take today to align your life with that vision?

_____

_____

What roles do self-care and personal growth play in your approach to aging?

How can you nurture your inner self as you age? What practices or habits can help you maintain mental and emotional well-being?

The Art of Growing Old

_____

_____

_____

_____

Reflect on how you can embrace and celebrate the wisdom and experiences you've gained over the years.

_____

_____

_____

_____

The Art of Growing Old

SECTION: II
Alone not lonely

In the grand play of life, losing people is a dramatic plot twist, not the final act!

The Art of Growing Old

Why I wanted to touch my toes

Our health is our wealth, as the adage goes! So true, so true. Even though we cannot take our healthy selves to the bank or sell our teeth, we know the opposite is detrimental. This means that having all the money in the world cannot add a tidbit to our longevity by itself. Our youthful years needed our health to make, spend, and save money — from muscle power to brain power. Even more so, we need our health during our senior years.

Senior years or retirement years can amount to over thirty additional years of life past our employment working life and it will really suck if after all that we have accomplished and faithfully fulfilled we end up spending most of that time unhealthy.

The Art of Growing Old

I grabbed this quotation from social media one day - "Enjoy every moment you have because in life, there are no rewinds, only flashbacks. Make sure it's all worth it." This point hits home all too solidly. During my 50s and into my 60s, I got that sensation often. The sensation of flashback to where I started to remember where I came from since I was in deep search of where I was going; in short, I was scared. I was afraid of the changes I was experiencing and wondered if I would be able to stay healthy as I got older. During those times in my early 50s, I suffered from a herniated disc and had to have lower back surgery.

Before going into surgery, I visited a therapist and started to prepare myself and my body for the changes that were coming. The therapist asked me what my biggest concern was, and in the presence of her assistant, I said I was not able to touch my toes without being in pain. The assistant asked me a tough thought-provoking question, 'why do you need to touch your toes?'

The question was baffling and I wondered how I would answer this assistant and why would such a question be asked? Everyone want to touch their toes I thought, it made me wonder how I was going to get through this? It made me wonder what I needed to do to maintain my health at that time and deep into my 50s, 60s and 70s. As of writing this, I am approaching sixty-two, my lower back is much better and sciatica completely gone. I can touch my toes, and I pray that everyone, as we get older strive to do the same.

Prior to getting healthier there were times I could not touch my toes and times where I could hardly stand up without excruciating pain but pushing myself past that limit was my goal and I'm very stubborn to accomplish goals. My late 50s were not going to be a time that I was going to struggle to put on clothes as I experienced.

Health and healthy living translate deeper into our sense of dignity. That sense of pride in us; the feeling of being worthy of honor or respect. It begins with self-respect and self-honor with the appropriate amount of dignity. To me, this is called mental health.

The Art of Growing Old

How to deal with frustrated family

A family with loving children is a blessing. However, the fact is as we begin living our 60s, our children are adults grappling with their own lives. As our physical and cognitive challenges rise, we cannot expect their tolerance index to rise. No matter how loving they are, practical everyday requirements may sour relationships.

Some family members do not give thought or consideration to the fact that we may be settled in our ways. At least that is what people call it. Many times, for lack of a better explanation, our behaviors are explained as being settled in our ways. I find it more accurate to say that we have to make tough and solid decisions, rather than frivolous ones, because of how quickly these decisions will impact our bottom line or well-being.

One of my friends, Cindy, said, "When you become frustrated with older people because of what they cannot do, think of how frustrated they must feel because they can no longer do it." This encapsulates the essence of the challenges seniors face. It beckons us to empathize with their perspective, acknowledging the impact of physical and cognitive limitations on their daily lives. Some family members may not fully comprehend the challenges they encounter. There is a lack of consideration for the fact that seniors may be settled in their ways due to the need for sound and decisive decision-making, rooted in a wealth of experience. While labeled as being "set in their ways," seniors may simply be drawing upon a lifetime of experiences to make informed choices that safeguard their well-being.

Differences in values, beliefs, and lifestyles between generations can lead to misunderstandings and frustrations. Seniors may feel disconnected from the younger generation's priorities, while the younger family members may struggle to relate to the experiences and perspectives of their elders. Seniors may feel a sense of disconnection from the younger generation's priorities, while their adult children may struggle to relate to the experiences and perspectives of their elders. I have noticed folks my age feel disconnected with youngsters, for multiple reasons, such as…

Cultural Shifts and Technological Divide:

The rapid pace of cultural and technological changes in recent decades has created a considerable gap between generations. Seniors may find it challenging to adapt to new technologies and evolving cultural norms, leading to a sense of alienation from the values and preferences of their adult children.

For instance, a senior may struggle to use social media platforms to stay in touch with family members who predominantly share updates and communicate through these digital channels. This can result in feelings of isolation as they may miss important family news and events. The terminology, etiquette, and pace of digital communication can be overwhelming, leading to a sense of disconnection.

Cultural norms and societal expectations have undergone significant shifts over the years. Seniors, shaped by the values of their era, may find it challenging to fully comprehend or embrace the changes in perspectives on topics such as gender roles, diversity, and individual freedoms. A senior who grew up in a more traditional setting may struggle to fully grasp the fluidity of gender roles and diverse family structures embraced by their adult children. This could lead to misunderstandings and a sense of alienation from the values that guide the younger generation.

Post-Covid, global events have accelerated the adoption of remote work and virtual interactions. A senior who is used to face-to-face interactions in the workplace may feel alienated when their adult children, working remotely, engage in virtual meetings and collaborate through digital platforms.

Similarly, the shift towards an increasingly digital economy has transformed the way financial transactions are conducted. Online banking, e-commerce, and digital payment systems have become the norm. A senior who prefers visiting a local bank branch for transactions may feel alienated when their adult children embrace online banking and digital payment apps. This divergence in financial practices can contribute to a sense of disconnection.

Differing Perspectives on Work:

This is a major conflicting point. Seniors, having grown up in a different economic landscape, may have distinct views on work, career, and retirement compared to their adult children. While the older generation may prioritize job stability and traditional career paths, younger family members might emphasize flexibility, entrepreneurship, or work-life balance.

This calls for a thoughtful and open-minded approach. Seniors can initiate constructive conversations with their adult children, aiming to understand the motivations behind their career choices. By actively listening to the younger generation's perspectives, seniors can gain insights into the changing dynamics of the contemporary workplace.

Encouraging an exchange of experiences and lessons learned from different eras can further strengthen family bonds, fostering a collaborative environment where both seniors and their adult children feel acknowledged and respected in their respective approaches to work and career.

Social and Political Ideologies:

Variations in social and political ideologies often emerge across generations. Seniors may hold beliefs shaped by historical events, while their adult children might be influenced by contemporary issues and evolving societal norms. These differences can lead to debates and conflicts on topics such as politics and social justice.

Seniors may have longstanding loyalty to specific political parties shaped by historical events or leaders who influenced their political views. These affiliations may be deeply rooted, contributing to resistance or skepticism towards newer political movements. For example, seniors who lived through transformative social movements, such as the civil rights era or feminist movements, may carry unique perspectives shaped by their participation or observation of these events. This can influence their stance on current social justice issues.

Encouraging conversations about the reasons behind differing ideologies fosters mutual understanding and strengthens the parent-children relationship. Seniors can acknowledge that the world their adult children navigate is distinct from their own and show a willingness to learn from each other. Given the years of experience, seniors are better placed to adopt a mindset that embraces the diversity of thought within the family. Seniors can encourage their adult children's civic engagement and activism.

Life Stage Priorities:

Seniors in their 60s may prioritize health, financial stability, and retirement planning, whereas their adult children might be more focused on career growth, raising children, and achieving a work-life balance.

A senior may dedicate more time to regular medical check-ups, exercise routines, and a balanced diet, while their adult child, juggling career demands and raising young children, may struggle to prioritize health with the same intensity, leading to potential misunderstandings.

A senior, having witnessed economic fluctuations over the years, may prioritize financial stability by focusing on savings, investments, and conservative spending. Their adult child, eager to advance in their career and provide immediate opportunities for their family, may lean towards spending on education, housing, and experiences, leading to conflicting views on financial priorities.

The adult child may be engrossed in the demanding responsibilities of raising young children, prioritizing their education, extracurricular activities, and overall well-being. Meanwhile, the senior, who has already navigated the challenges of parenthood, may unintentionally downplay the urgency of certain parenting decisions, leading to misunderstandings.

Seniors can strike a balance between prioritizing their health and financial stability while respecting and supporting career growth and family-building efforts of their adult children. This collaborative approach fosters harmony within the family.

By listening actively to the concerns, ideas, and experiences of their adult children, seniors can demonstrate respect for their perspectives and reinforce a sense of validation, even if there are differing opinions.

Cultivating a habit of engaging in shared activities can appeal to multiple generations. This not only helps bring adult children closer, but also grandkids. Exploring new hobbies together and engaging in family traditions are great bridges.

Finally, it is extremely important to acknowledge the autonomy and independence of adult children. It augurs well for us to remember our younger days. How we sought to have space and freedom from our parents. Seniors should respect the decisions and choices of their younger family members. Recognize that each generation brings unique perspectives, and diversity can enrich family dynamics rather than create divisions.

In the worst cases, do not hesitate to seek professional guidance. If communication breakdowns persist, consider seeking the assistance of a family counselor or mediator. Professional guidance can facilitate constructive conversations, provide strategies for conflict resolution, and help family members understand each other better.

The Art of Growing Old

How to deal with loss of friends

Similarly, friendships once abundant in the workplace or local communities may dwindle after retirement, and if there are any left. That being said, for many, friends are really associates. Associates we worked with, or people we interacted with in the proximity of where we live.

When we get older many take decisions to move away, or move into smaller accommodations, which would cause them to evaluate what location they decide to live in upon retirement. The group of associates that we would spend many hours with at work has dwindled down to maybe none so we may get a feeling that we do not have any friends or true friends, especially if we did not solidify that during the working years or if we did not move to a location familiar to us and our associated friends.

Depending on how it turns out, retirement could be a point of continuation or a point of starting over. If we move away from our location to downsize as it were, we may have to start collecting an assortment of friends when you get the opportunity to start from the beginning again.

The significance of having good friends in the post-retirement phase cannot be overstated. Meaningful friendships contribute to a fulfilling and emotionally rich life, offering numerous benefits for seniors, such as…

Emotional Support:

Good friends provide a crucial source of emotional support, helping seniors navigate the various challenges that may arise during retirement, such as adjusting to lifestyle changes or dealing with health issues. Good friendships reduce the risk of social isolation and thereby improve overall well-being and mental health.

Shared Hobbies:

Friends offer companionship for shared activities and hobbies, bringing joy and fulfillment to daily life. Engaging in interests together promotes a sense of purpose and enjoyment. Friends of the same age group understand one another better, they share similar values and have a similar outlook on life in general, providing one another a comfort net.

Community Engagement:

Seniors can always cultivate new friendships in retirement. By engaging with local community groups, clubs, or volunteer organizations, they can meet like-minded individuals and build new friendships.

Similarly, participating in social events, community gatherings, or activities tailored to specific interests provides opportunities to connect with others who share similar passions.

Many communities have senior centers that organize social activities and events. Joining these centers provides a chance to meet new people and cultivate friendships.

People around would appreciate it if a senior were to take the lead and set up local clubs. Be that hiking or walking club, music club, book club, art & craft club, cooking club, photography club, writing club, travel enthusiasts club, etc.

Exercise Your Brain:

Embracing technology is an easy way today to foster cognitive engagement. I can vouch for this from personal experience. Especially after I started my podcast [Free Talk with Mr. B], I have made friends from across continents. Online platforms, social media, and community forums can help seniors find and connect with individuals who share common interests.

Engage your mind, learn new things. Our brain is a muscle. If you let it stay idle, it stagnates, crippling you. One can learn new things at any age. So, enroll in classes or workshops on topics of interest, which can lead to interactions with peers who have similar passions, fostering the development of meaningful connections.

Making Younger Friends:

Have you thought about making friends across age boundaries? Interact and spend time with the younger lot to add richness and vibrancy to your new phase in life.

You can find them in local community events or festivals where people of all ages come together.

Explore volunteer opportunities with organizations or causes that resonate with you. Volunteering often involves working with diverse groups, fostering connections with individuals of varying ages. Whether it's art, music, or a recreational activity, engaging in shared interests within your community or church can be a catalyst for building friendships. Participating in fitness or wellness groups, such as yoga classes or walking clubs will also help seniors meet individuals of different ages, providing a natural setting for social interaction.

Younger friends bring fresh perspectives, introducing you to new ideas, trends, and cultural influences. Interacting with younger individuals can provide mental stimulation, keeping your mind active and engaged with contemporary thoughts and discussions. They help you understand technological advancements, helping you stay connected in the digital age.

The active lifestyles of younger friends can motivate and inspire seniors to stay physically active and explore new activities. Connecting with younger individuals contributes to an increased sense of social connectedness. Also, as a retiree, your life experiences and wisdom can serve as valuable contributions to the lives of younger friends, creating a sense of legacy and purpose. Do not lose an opportunity to share your expertise and experiences. Younger individuals may appreciate guidance, and this can pave the way for meaningful connections. You may also find an alternative income source [More about this in later chapters]. Most importantly, if you have lost your long-time partner, younger friends can help you heal faster.

It's a life-time partnership

The loss of a life partner can be a profound and life-altering event, requiring individuals to navigate grief, redefine their sense of self, and adjust to a changed reality. Can we even prepare for such a phase? I have no clear answer. Accepting the universal truth that no one escapes alive is but just the beginning. I have seen loved ones in my family navigating through this loss. Each one has their own coping mechanism, and the best support would be to give the individual the space while we stand close-by for any help.

Serving as a patient listener, I have seen, always works wonders. Sit beside and simply listen. Give them hugs. Silent hugs. No words can heal them or console them. Especially, if it has been a long marriage, then the partners become a habit for each other. You have no authority or expertise to instruct them on how to move forward.

Based on conversations with individuals who have experienced the loss of their partners, the emotional and mental journey of a surviving spouse after losing a long-time partner is deeply nuanced and personal. The insights shared reveal a wide range of experiences, underscoring the complexity of grief.

Here is a compilation of their sentiments:

Grief, marked by intense sadness and sorrow, is a common thread in these conversations. This natural process allows individuals to grapple with the profound reality of losing a beloved partner. The initial stages often involve shock and disbelief, especially when the loss is sudden or unexpected. The full weight of the situation may take time to sink in.

Feelings of loneliness emerge prominently as the absence of a long-time spouse disrupts shared lives, companionship, and daily routines that were once central to existence. Deep anguish and heartache are prevalent emotions as individuals navigate the emotional pain of losing someone they loved deeply, leading to periods of sadness and, in some cases, depression.

In certain situations, a complex interplay of relief and guilt arises. Relief may stem from the end of a partner's suffering, while guilt accompanies the natural questioning of one's emotional responses. Numbness becomes a coping mechanism for some, as emotional detachment serves as a shield against overwhelming grief during certain phases of the mourning process. Feelings of regret and contemplation of what-ifs are common as surviving spouses grapple with the complexities of the grieving process, replaying moments in their minds.

The loss can trigger an identity crisis, with the roles and responsibilities tied to the partnership leaving the surviving spouse questioning their sense of self in the absence of their partner. Over time, some individuals express reaching a stage of acceptance and adjustment to life without their spouse. This is not about forgetting but finding a way to move forward.

A few of them found seeking support from friends, family, or grief support groups a vital part of the healing process. Talking about the loss and sharing emotions serves as a therapeutic outlet.

Memorializing and honoring the late spouse become essential aspects of the healing journey for some. Creating tributes, participating in rituals, and engaging in activities to honor their memory contribute to the healing process.

It's crucial to acknowledge that there is no one-size-fits-all approach to grief, and seeking professional support, such as counseling or therapy, proves beneficial for those navigating the complex emotions associated with the loss of a longtime spouse.

Celebrating the life of a departed partner is a meaningful way to honor their memory. Here are some ways I have seen individuals celebrate their departed partner's life:

Creating a Memory Book:
Compiling photographs, letters, and mementos to create a memory book that captures the essence of your partner's life.

Hosting a Memorial Event:
Organizing a memorial event where friends and family can gather to share stories, memories, and celebrate the positive impact the partner had on others' lives.

Contributing to a Cause:

Contributing to a cause or charity that was important to your partner. This could be a way to continue their legacy and make a positive impact.

Planting a Memorial Garden:

Planting a garden or dedicating a tree in memory of your partner. It can serve as a living tribute and a place for reflection.

Creating an Annual Tradition:

Establish an annual tradition or ritual to commemorate special occasions or milestones related to your partner.

Writing a Letter:

Write a letter to your departed partner expressing your feelings, gratitude, and memories. This can be a cathartic and personal way to celebrate their life.

Celebrating a departed partner's life has several positives. It helps shift the focus from mourning the loss to honoring the positive aspects of their existence. It can contribute to the healing process and provide a sense of closure, allowing for a healthier grieving experience. When celebration involves others, it fosters a sense of connection and support within a community and contributes to preserving their legacy. Ultimately, whether through mourning or celebrating, the key is to allow yourself the time and space to grieve in a way that feels authentic to you. The process of returning to a comfortable routine is unique for each individual.

Setting stage for the final act

We plan for our old age, but how many plan beyond that. When should one think of estate planning and make end-of-life decisions? Is there a right time at all? Most people tend to avoid this for varied reasons.

The common reason I see is the discomfort in the idea of facing one's own death. Death is the only truth of our life that we know for sure will happen. So, it's only wise for us, as we step into our senior age, to make humor our companion and sort serious matters with a chuckle. Laughter in ample doses will make medicines work their magic. Estate planning is an opportunity to bring some fun to our life story. I'd love for my family to have a good laugh after the tears they shed for me.

Another reason people may delay taking action is the fear of loss of control. Some people feel by creating an end-of-life plan they are giving up control over their assets or decisions, even though the purpose is to ensure their wishes are respected. Not to mention the complexity and cumbersome legal documentation, and not fully understanding legal terms or the fear of making mistakes. This is where it is important for us to understand that taking help is a natural progression of life.

As we mentioned earlier, financial stability plays a significant role in some seniors avoiding taking such decisions. Investing in professional advice for planning can be expensive. So let's plan for having the funds in place as we step into our senior age. And hope we have the wisdom to sort out family dynamics, because complicated family relationships or unresolved issues may make discussing end-of-life decisions and estate planning uncomfortable.

As much as we acknowledge the universal truth of mortality, we often believe there is plenty of time left and thus put off planning, especially in the absence of immediate health concerns. Even as life expectancy rates have increased today, unexpected deaths post-COVID are also a new reality. I know people who trust that default legal and healthcare systems will adequately handle their affairs without the need for specific plans. Maybe they will, but why leave things to chance? Having a personal plan allows for more control, customization, and fewer hassles for your loved ones after you pass.

Estate Planning:

The Will is your paramount script of life. You've journeyed through life, amassing memories, possessions, and maybe even a peculiar assortment of antique teapots. Now, it's the moment to ensure that these treasures find their way to the perfect recipients after your final chapter unfolds.

Estate planning is like directing the big ending of your life story. Imagine it as creating your masterpiece, your most important creation, where you get to choose who gets the family heirloom like that vintage guitar your brother played in his younger days, or the old family recipe book filled with cherished memories. It's your opportunity to prevent the confusion and mistakes that happen when there's no plan in place. Estate planning is your chance to avoid mix-ups and make sure everything goes smoothly. So, picture it as setting the stage for a play – you're the director, and you decide who gets the lead role and who helps with the props. It's your way of making sure everyone knows their part and everything goes according to plan, of saying, 'I had a good run; I left them with a smile, right until the very end'.

Power of Attorney:

Of course, one can use the power of attorney. It is a sort-of-reliable backup. This document allows someone you trust to make decisions for you if you can't. It's a bit like having a backup director for those times when life throws unexpected challenges your way and you can't be there. But keep in mind, having a power of attorney isn't an excuse for wild decision-making. It's more like passing the director's role to a trusted assistant who knows when to start things and when to stop them.

Healthcare Directives:

It's great if you have a trusted aide, especially in the scenario where one develops cognitive challenges. However, let's plan in advance and have advanced healthcare directives in place. This document allows you to specify your preferences regarding medical treatments when you can't voice them yourself. It's your chance to be the star of your own show, dictating whether you want an elaborate special effects sequence or a simple fade to black.

Funeral Planning:

This is the elephant in the room, no one likes to speak about it. It may stir up deep emotions, causing anxiety, sadness, or even guilt. Seniors might avoid these discussions to shield themselves from emotional distress. Planning for your funeral is something we all can do to exit in style by leaving our mark. Some people avoid this conversation but think of it as an opportunity to organize a memorable farewell event. Do you envision a quiet and reflective gathering, or perhaps a lively celebration completes with confetti cannons? It's entirely up to you.

Most of us adhere to cultural and religious influences. But if you are a fun-loving person, this is your last chance to have your way. Consider adding a personal touch – maybe suggest a dress code where everyone wears your favorite color or create a slideshow showcasing your most amusing moments.

Keep in mind, it's your last chance to make an impression, and you get to be in charge. Make it special, and who knows, your funeral might be the talk of the afterlife town!

The Art of Growing Old

Purpose, passion & personal priority

Entering the senior phase of life, post 60 years of age, can be a transformative experience. While it often brings a sense of wisdom, accomplishment, and the freedom to explore new facets of life, it may also present challenges, particularly the risk of loneliness. It's important for us to distinguish between feeling lonely and feeling alone, and to understand how each situation affects us emotionally.

Being alone and feeling lonely are entirely two distinct concepts. I consider myself a people's person. I love interacting with people of all ages, however, I also like my solitude, where I can recharge myself and immerse myself in activities that I love. Many seniors find joy and fulfillment in solitude, relishing the freedom to explore personal interests, hobbies, and reflective moments, after having spent decades in jobs taking up liabilities and responsibilities.

Loneliness is a subjective emotional state that arises when an individual perceives a lack of meaningful connections. The key to embracing seniority lies in finding a balance between solitude and social engagement, while taking care of one's well-being. Exercising regularly, eating well, and getting enough sleep will help us stay healthy overall. Also, trying out calming activities like meditation and yoga can help us handle stress and keep a positive attitude.

As we grow older, things will change, and that's okay. It means accepting that our body might not do everything it used to. But it also means finding happiness in new things we can do. Focusing on what we can control, making small changes to our routine, and trying to see the good in each moment is great. But what is more important in senior ages is to find a meaning to our life.

People call it many names - purpose, passion, calling. That's our personal choice and definition. For me my purpose, passion and calling at this phase in my life is to 'GIVE BACK' – give back to humanity and myself. I am focused on being my best version by prioritizing myself and my needs so that I can help as many as I can. I have taken to riding, podcasting, writing, and consulting. If you haven't yet found your purpose, here's a checklist that can help you…

Reflect on Past Experiences:

Consider past experiences, both personal and professional, which were rewarding and challenging, to identify patterns and lessons learned. This will help you identify your skills, and the impact you've had on others.

Explore New Hobbies and Interests:

Attempt to do new activities. Revisit hobbies you had as a youngster in school/college. What are the things that sparked your curiosity then? Rekindle your old dreams; those which you put on the back burner. Attend workshops to discover new interests and meet like-minded individuals. Or use technology and update your skills and hobbies. There is nothing that is not available online today.

Identify Core Values:

List out the principles and values that have stood you in good stead and consider how they can be used to fulfill your future needs. Volunteer for causes that align with your values. Helping others achieve their dreams is not only fulfilling but also eye-opening. It can lead you to discover your hidden skills and talents.

While you are doing all these, remember to set realistic goals. It is common for us seniors to overdo things to validate ourselves. Define clear, achievable goals that align with your newfound interests or calling and break down larger goals into smaller, manageable steps.

Seek Professional Guidance:

There's no age limit or shame in seeking help. Consult with career counselors, life coaches, or mentors who can provide insights. Professional advice can help you navigate the process of discovering your purpose or defining your passion or crafting your calling. Finally, accept the fact that purpose can evolve over time. So be open to adjusting goals and priorities as your interests and circumstances change.

Afterall, we are on an individual journey and bringing a sense of meaning to our life is a sacred and personal mission – to each his own. Let us be our own benchmark!

MINDFUL MUSINGS

Reflect on a time when you felt alone but not lonely. What activities or mindsets helped you embrace solitude?

_____

_____

_____

_____

_____

How can you cultivate a sense of contentment and fulfillment when you are alone?

_____

_____

_____

_____

What motivates you to maintain physical health as you age? How do you incorporate physical activity into your daily routine?

What are your physical health goals, and how do they contribute to your overall well-being and happiness?

_____

_____

How do you manage conflicts or frustrations within your family? What strategies have you found effective in maintaining harmony?

_____

_____

_____

_____

What steps can you take to foster understanding and patience in family relationships as you age?

_____

_____

Reflect on the impact of losing friends. How do you cope with the grief and continue to find joy in life?

How can you build and nurture new relationships as you age to combat loneliness and stay socially active?

What does a lifetime partnership mean to you, and how do you nurture your relationship with your spouse?

How can you and your spouse support each other's personal growth and happiness as you both age?

_____

_____

_____

How do you want to be remembered, and what steps can you take to ensure your legacy lives on?

_____

_____

_____

_____

What practical and emotional preparations can you make to help your loved ones cope after you are gone?

_____

_____

_____

_____

_____

What are your current passions, and how do they contribute to your sense of purpose and fulfillment?

_____

_____

_____

_____

How do you prioritize your personal well-being and happiness in your daily life?

_____

_____

Reflect on a moment when you felt deeply passionate about something. How did it impact your sense of purpose and motivation?

How can you align your daily activities with your passions to create a more fulfilling life as you age?

How can you ensure that your personal priorities are respected and maintained even as you navigate the changes and challenges of aging?

ID## The Art of Growing Old

SECTION: III
Rekindling Passion

Post-career, hobbies breathe life into dormant childhood aspirations

The Art of Growing Old

A Trinidadian's green thumb

It is often said, "the more things change, the more they stay the same". I look back at my life and wonder how life played out. As a young man, I loved gardening, born and raised in the countryside of the island nation of Trinidad and Tobago. While in high school on the island of St Croix in the United States Virgin Islands, one of my favorite classes, of many non-academic requirements, gave me the feeling and emotional connection to the earth.

I was captivated reading Marcus Tullius Cicero's '*How to Grow Old - Ancient Wisdom for the Second Half of Life*' [translated in a 2016 copyrighted version by Philip Freeman]. In one of the chapters he writes, "What delights me are not only the fruits of the land but the power and nature of the earth itself. It receives the scattered seed in its softened and ready womb, and for a time the seed remains hidden — *occaecatum* in Latin, hence our word occatio. Then warmed by the moist heat of its embrace, the seed expands and brings forth a green and flourishing blade. With the support of its fibrous roots, it grows and matures until at last it stands erect on its jointed stalk. Now within its sheath it has reached its adolescent stage so that finally it bursts forth and an ear of grain comes into the light with ordered rows and a palisade of spikes as protection against nibbling by small birds."

How romantic! What pleasure, what delight! I told my farm partners in Nigeria that I will not put my hand out too soon. When I get old, I will return to reap the rewards from the earth. This 2013 statement holds true to date, since the farm is still going strong, and I am not old enough yet.

In life's journey, there's a beauty in the cycle that mirrors the earth's nurturing process. Our professional years are like the seed tucked in the soil, unseen yet full of potential. Just as the earth cradles the seed in its warm embrace, our experiences and efforts during our working years prepare us for growth. Retirement, then, becomes a season of rediscovery—a time to plant new seeds, reviving long-forgotten passions that have been patiently waiting in the soil of our souls.

The Art of Growing Old

As we step into this new phase, it's like witnessing the sprouting of a green blade. The support of our life's experiences acts as roots, providing stability and strength. Retirement becomes a time to stand tall, much like the mature plant swaying in the breeze. The unfolding of this chapter is akin to the plant bursting forth, revealing the ear of grain—a symbol of the ordered rows of new pursuits and the protective palisade against the nibbles of doubt and hesitation.

Our life's path, much like the growth of the plant, is a testament to the power and resilience within us. Each phase, from hidden seed to mature stalk, contributes to our life story, reminding us that every moment, whether in the soil of work or the sunshine of retirement, plays a vital role in the beauty of our unfolding story.

In the meantime, I farm at my US home, in the back yard due to that sense of desire for completion, the desire for connection. Yet, it's my aging process that truly connects me with the romance of Marcus Tullius Cicero's writings about the connection between us growing old and valuing the love for farming – the love of the fruits of the earth!

Engaging in farming during our golden years presents a myriad of emotional and mental benefits. Tending to a garden or cultivating a small farm not only reconnects us with the earth but also serves as a therapeutic outlet, reducing stress and promoting a sense of tranquility. The rhythmic, hands-on nature of farming provides a meditative space, allowing us to escape the hustle of daily life and find solace in the simple yet profound acts of planting, nurturing, and harvesting. Furthermore, the act of witnessing the fruits of our labor offers a tangible sense of accomplishment, boosting self-esteem and fostering a positive mindset. If we were to pause and reflect, we can see how the cycle of growth and renewal mirrors the seasons of our life, allowing us to accept change better.

In addition to the emotional and mental well-being derived from the process, there's the added benefit of regular physical activity, promoting mobility and fitness. I would call farming and gardening a therapeutic embrace in retirement years.

I'm a star playing house at 60

What is this? Seriously? Why? We may ask. Yet, it can be very satisfying and rewarding. Rewarding from a completely different angle; from a completely different perspective.

As someone who loves making a home feel special, I help my wife Han in the kitchen, carefully setting up everything – from the neatly arranged utensils to the shiny countertops. Making my morning coffee feels like a little ritual, exquisite mugs, chosen with care for their quality and elegance. Our cups are a testament to our appreciation for the finer things, reflecting our shared love for all that is tasteful and refined. It's about savoring the simple joys in life with a touch of class. When I prepare lunch for us, it's not just about food; it's about creating a beautiful experience.

I pick out ingredients with care, set the table thoughtfully, and choose elegant plates and glasses. The whole process is like an art project, making my home a cozy place where everything has its own tidy spot.

In my world, even the smallest details matter. Plates, glasses, beds, furniture are more than just things. They are chosen with love to add a touch of elegance to each day. It's not about being fancy; it's about appreciating the simple joy of living well. My home becomes a canvas where every day is a chance to create a little masterpiece of order, style, and warmth. This is playing house for me at my age.

As kids or in our youth we participated in playing house as an activity, at times reluctantly, because we wanted to fit in; we wanted to emulate what we were first exposed to. We wanted to try it out since it's what we first saw. As we get older or in retirement and senior years, we get to playhouse with the stars. For whatever reason, hotels and restaurants are rated with stars.

So why not go all out and be a 'star'. Playing house as an older person is an opportunity to create a home, a five-star or six-star setting over dinner or to maintain our accommodation to the highest level of affordability we can get.

I am not talking about the car or modes of transportation here. I am talking about that feeling we had as children. The feeling of actually drinking tea. The idea of having the dishes lined up and by old age; not pretending to have the exquisite delight in the abundance of foods but to have the foods we prefer in good measure.

Fantasy, you say? Why, yes… the fantasy and passion associated with every bite.

Playing house is learning how to make the bed up the way you like. Playing house is hanging the towels in the way that you would see it in the most expensive hotel. Playing house is keeping things neat and clean just the way you would've wanted it. Playing house is getting completely dressed up and going nowhere other than to the dinner table each time.

This sense of satisfaction is highly appreciated, and I would venture to say that it is mostly appreciated during our older ages when we have that strong desire to smell the roses in appreciation of them just being there.

We often times use the phrase, 'there is no place like home', as we get older and older, the phrase takes on more significance than ever and it's in our best interest to assist the home to be that by actually playing house. It would have been really nice to get all these feelings and emotions during youth. Plus, I'm not suggesting some do not. What I am saying is that playing house and participating in all aspects of maintaining and sustaining a NPLH (No Place Like Home) activity can add to the gracefulness of aging.

The act of playing house in our senior years is a powerful and transformative experience. It transcends the mundane and transforms our living spaces into havens of personal expression. As we meticulously arrange our homes, set tables with care, and revel in the simple delights of a well-made bed, the emotional and mental benefits become increasingly evident.

Engaging in the art of playing house offers a profound sense of purpose for seniors. It is a daily practice that goes beyond mere chores; it becomes a therapeutic outlet for self-expression and creativity. The deliberate choices made in decorating, organizing, and curating one's living environment provide a sense of control and agency, fostering a positive mindset and boosting self-esteem.

Playing house not only serves as a gateway to nostalgia, connecting us with the joyous simplicity of our youth, but also becomes a profound expression of identity in our senior years. The ability to create and maintain a home that aligns with personal tastes and preferences serves as a source of pride and fulfillment.

Playing house is not just a physical activity; it is a powerful elixir for the mind and soul, enriching the golden years with purpose, joy, and a celebration of the art of living well.

The Art of Growing Old

Be a new you

The water was deep, and fear gripped me as I descended into its mysterious abyss. The weight of uncertainty hung heavy, my heart pounding in my mouth with each breath. But I could hear instructions. As I adjusted to the alien environment, the fear slowly ebbed away. The serenity of the underwater realm embraced me, and the beauty of its vibrant inhabitants took my breath away in a different, more wondrous way. I found calmness, felt excitement, and sensed profound relaxation as I surrendered to the mysteries of the deep. I knew I was safe. I was safe!

Fifty years ago, when I jumped into the water, I had no manual, no one to give me instructions. I was barely in my teens when I learned to float—float in life! So much so that the 12-year-old me soon mastered the art of diving into every challenge, maneuvering through every unknown curve, and keeping myself, my mother, my partner, my kids, my friends, and my colleagues afloat. I made every soul that crossed my path feel safe and loved. I gave it all for more than five decades. Now, in the latter period of my life here, as I turn to give back to myself, in order to fill my cup to continue giving to others, I attempted Scuba Diving.

Now is the time for us to finally do all the things we've always wanted to do but couldn't before. However, we should be careful not to put ourselves in danger, especially because at this age, physical harm can be really serious. I did my best studying the equipment section in the book and the safe practices for being under water using breathing air. It was only when I felt confident having the knowledge that I decided to take the dive.

It was exhilarating because it turned out that my imagination may have gotten the best of me. The first part of the pool was actually three feet, and the trainer was right there to guide me. By the second day we were in the 14-feet section of the same pool learning to become buoyant and I had an a-ha moment. Some things are great to learn early in life and some things need life to help you learn even if it's not early. The lesson here is to just keep breathing. That was also the number one rule in the diving book - to 'always keep breathing'. When I concentrated only on my breathing, the water no longer was mysterious, no longer was alien, no longer was I gripped with fear. All we need to do is keep breathing underwater and in life!

As fine wine gets better with age, so do we. We have the experience and wisdom to take risks safely. Age brings mental resilience and perspective, says author Jojo Moyes, who achieved an impressive feat by winning her inaugural dressage competition at the age of 54. Despite facing arduous training that initially made her contemplate quitting due to concerns about her age and fragility, Moyes adopted a perspective of viewing it as a gradual process. Focusing on incremental improvements played a crucial role in sustaining her commitment.

According to Moyes, maturity comes from an enhanced ability to rationalize situations, acknowledging that making mistakes is not catastrophic. She says senior people have the advantage of increased willpower, emphasizing the necessity of putting in dedicated training hours.

As we age, our perspective on life changes, offering opportunities to learn and re-learn what achievements and success mean. Comparing ourselves to others may not be as straightforward as in disciplines like dressage or ballet on horseback, but we can focus on the details as we navigate the new perspectives that come with growing older.

Success in these endeavors demands patience and meticulous attention to details. While in our youth, we might have noticed highlights in someone's hair, with age, we tend to appreciate those highlights differently. There's a shift towards honoring the crown of wisdom in someone's hair as we mature.

Back in the day, I loved tearing it up on motorbikes. But, you know, life happened, and I couldn't hit the pedals as much as I wanted. Got caught up dealing with the whole manly responsibility gig – in the midst of providing and earning a living, bikes had to take a back seat.

Post active-professional years, I've resurrected my trusty bike from the garage. We're talking about some serious bike servicing action. Got that baby tuned up and ready to roll. As a precautionary measure, I took classes, too. Now, I'm hitting the road for some epic long drives, soaking in the breeze and soaking up that sweet sunshine. It's like a reunion with my two-wheeled buddy after a long hiatus.

The Art of Growing Old

When I'm cruising on those long rides, it's pure bliss. The wind in my face, the sun kissing my skin – it's the ultimate stress buster. No more worrying about the daily grind; it's just me, the road, and the thrill of the ride. It's like therapy on two wheels. Do you feel me?

Reviving my love for riding has become my secret to staying refreshed and feeling youthful. It's not just about exercise; it's a journey reclaiming a youthful spirit, offering mental well-being, physical health, and the freedom retirement deserves.

So, if you have a bike, grab that bike and hit the road, if you have a sport that you played in your younger days, take that up, if you love outdoors hike, trek, run that marathon [if your knees are not cooperating, walk along, but don't park your dream aside anymore] - it's the golden ticket to a vibrant retirement. **Returning** to activities that you once enjoyed opens the door to discovering a new you within yourself, unlocking hidden potentials and igniting a sense of renewed vitality.

The Art of Growing Old

I'm no Rapunzel in the digital era

So, I was turning 60 when I had an a-ha moment. I was sitting in this iconic tower, the Burj Khalifa in Dubai. The 17th floor apartment facing eastward was amazingly beautiful with stunning views of the sunrise. Although they seeded the clouds on occasion, it seemed as if they were seeded just for me to see each morning as the sun rays created the most amazing rays of light with each passing moment.

Yet, the moments were indeed passing and the feeling of being asked to work from home was not a feeling desired at 60. There was never going to be a moment to rewind. Never an opportunity to do over. Never to get young again; only to walk slowly into that good night.

Giving thought to the fact that all I would be able to do was to look back to reminisce on how I spent the time, I knew I had to do something, I knew I had to make sure it was all worth it. The idea of getting to 60 and stuck in a Rapunzel-like tower was not for me. No way was I going to grow blond hair and definitely not let down my hair so that anyone can climb up. The idea kept me thinking about what I could do and the a-ha moment hit me.

I realized that I had lots of advantages, gathered throughout my six decades, especially becoming an authority on a variety of topics. Experiences were sitting smack in our frontal lobe accumulated over so many years and potential ready to share; ready to give back to as many as possible. Why not start a podcast? I mused one day, realizing the immense potential of embracing technology in my senior years. In this digital age, launching a podcast seemed like the perfect way to stay current and relevant.

The thought of diving into the world of microphones and online platforms felt like an exciting adventure. It wasn't just about keeping up with the times; it's about carving out a space to share wisdom, experiences, and life stories. It's not just about staying active in the digital era; it's about becoming digital storytellers, weaving our unique narratives in a way only seniors can.

So, let's break the stereotype that technology is for the younger generation. Seniors starting podcasts isn't just about embracing the present; it's about crafting a legacy, leaving behind a digital footprint that reflects the class, wisdom, and stylish experiences of our golden years. In the world of podcasts, age becomes a badge of honor, and every senior has a story worth sharing. And thus I started my podcast 'Free Talk With Mr. B'. Also, the philosophy centers on the idea of giving a person a fish versus teaching them how to fish. If we give cash or other valuables, someone will eat today. However, teaching someone how to fish or sharing experiences and providing motivational guidance can help them eat every day.

Bringing stories of people to a wider audience gives them hope and the needed stimulation to keep going. And I did this while sitting at home in Dubai. It is what they called 'working from home' wondering when everything will get back to normal; wondering what action to take if and when being stuck inside would ever end. As a senior, the journey into podcasting has been more than just emulation; it has been an enlightening process of learning and growth. Immersing myself in the world of podcasting required overcoming technological hurdles, a challenge I confronted with determination and sought guidance from those well-versed in the field. This learning experience not only enhanced my technical knowledge but also fostered a sense of accomplishment in conquering new skills as a senior.

Podcasting has been like a key for my mind and emotions. I am reminded of Daniel Levitin, a professor of neuroscience at McGill University, who challenged the assumption that aging inevitably leads to cognitive and physical decline in his book *The Changing Mind*. He argues that our societal perspective is rooted in prejudice rather than science. Contrary to common belief, Levitin emphasizes that the capacity for learning and forming new brain connections persists throughout life.

I can vouch for this. Podcasting post age-60 is more than just sharing my thoughts – it's like opening a door to understanding people's worries and problems from all sorts of jobs and places. Talking with guests and having deep chats has made me see things in a new way, giving me good ideas and making me feel connected to others, no matter their age or background.

Doing podcasts taught me that being a senior is about more than just learning tech stuff; it's about discovering the many stories' people have, and every episode is like a new chapter where I learn and understand a bit more.

It's crucial to recognize that technology is not age-restricted; rather, it is a tool that can be adapted to suit individual needs, preferences, and interests. By dispelling the bias that tech is exclusively for the young, seniors can open the door to a world of opportunities that contribute to mental stimulation and overall well-being.

Ask yourself how you can give back using technology. How you can share your wisdom, your experience using technology. Here are a few ideas you may want to explore…

Blogging:

Starting a blog is like having an online diary where seniors can share their stories, thoughts, and what they know with people from all over the world. For example, a retired teacher might write about the best ways to teach or share memories from their long career.

Online Forums and Communities:

Seniors can join online groups that match their interests. By talking and giving advice, they can share what they know. Imagine a retired gardener sharing gardening tips with an online group of plant enthusiasts.

Video Sharing:

Making and sharing videos on websites like YouTube is a way for seniors to show what they're good at. For example, a retired chef might make videos about cooking or share their kitchen wisdom with others.

Online Classes:

Seniors can use websites like Udemy or Coursera to create and teach classes about things they love. For instance, if someone knows a lot about languages, they could make a class to teach others.

Social Media Participation:

Being active on social media means seniors can talk to more people. They can share what they know, join conversations, and be part of a bigger group. Like, an artist can post their artwork on Instagram or Pinterest or TikTok.

Mentoring Programs:

Joining programs that connect seniors with people who want to learn from them is a great way to share knowledge. For instance, a retired person who worked in HR might help someone with their career through a mentoring program.

Telling Stories Online:

Seniors can use websites that help them tell their stories with pictures and words. This could be making a presentation with photos or writing about their life on sites like StoryCorps or Our Life Logs.

Writing Together:

Seniors can work with others to write articles for websites or newspapers. A retired journalist might share their opinions by writing pieces for online publications.

Speaking to a Group Online:

Using the internet, seniors can talk to a lot of people at once in online events or conferences. This is like speaking to a big audience. A retired motivational speaker might continue to inspire others by speaking to groups through the internet.

The write act beyond retirement

The phrase 'the art of getting old' often refers to growing old gracefully, as noted by many pundits. Yet, we all do not really apply that gracefulness with all we do. We are motivated by too many different 'just don't die' approaches. I often times find quotes that attempt to motivate our aging consciousness with reminders such as CS Lewis' - 'You are never too old to set another goal' or 'dream a new dream'. In case you're worried that you missed out on life, you didn't; if a 102-year-old lady can go skydiving, you can build your business. Our thoughts are our only barrier.

Peter Mark Roget, a British physician, natural theologian, and lexicographer, created Roget's Thesaurus at the age of 73. He began compiling in 1805 and the first edition of the Thesaurus was published in 1852. He continued to work on and expand subsequent editions until his death.

The Art of Growing Old

Harry Bernstein was a British-born American author who gained widespread recognition for his late literary debut. Bernstein achieved literary fame with his first book, *The Invisible Wall: A Love Story That Broke Barriers*, which was published when he was 96 years old. He continued to write, until he passed away on June 3, 2011, at the age of 101, leaving behind a literary legacy that defied traditional age-related expectations in the world of publishing.

Charles Darwin, renowned English naturalist, geologist, and biologist is best known for his groundbreaking work on the theory of evolution by natural selection. Darwin published his seminal work, *On the Origin of Species by Means of Natural Selection*, or the *Preservation of Favored Races in the Struggle for Life*, at age 50. He continued to publish works related to evolution, in his later years.

Laura Ingalls Wilder, an American writer, is best known for her *Little House* series of children's books, which are based on her childhood experiences in the American Midwest during the late 19th century. Her first book, *Little House in the Big Woods*, was published in 1932 when she was 65 years old. The success of the initial book led to a series of eight books that chronicled her life and adventures.

The Art of Growing Old

Colonel Sanders, born in 1890, had various jobs before opening a service station during the Great Depression. Only at age 62, in 1952, did he start franchising KFC. Facing challenges, he retained control in Canada and sold the company for $2 million at age 73 in 1964. Despite achieving fame late, Sanders remained a public figure through commercials until his death in 1980.

As I looked at the stories of these late bloomers, I realized that age is not a barrier to meaningful accomplishments. So, at the age of 60, I embarked on writing my first book, *The Art of Giving Back*.

This endeavor was more than just leaving a legacy for my family; it was a platform to share the invaluable lessons from my life journey and inspire the younger generation to embrace life's challenges.

The Art of Giving Back became a tribute to my mother, an expression of love for my siblings, and a profound way of giving back to the world. Little did I know that this writing journey would transform my life in unexpected ways. It became an emotional exploration, a reflection on my formative years, and a powerful tool to reshape my perspective on relationships.

Through the process, I found a deeper connection with my son. Writing allowed me to view myself from a distance, gaining insights that only retrospection could provide. Now, armed with the wisdom acquired through documenting my life, I am better equipped to offer advice to the younger generation, encouraging them not to give up in the face of challenges.

To all seniors, I extend a heartfelt call to capture their life moments in a book. It is a journey that goes beyond leaving a legacy; it is a therapeutic exploration that brings about personal growth, emotional healing, and a renewed sense of purpose. As we share our stories, we not only enrich the lives of others but also find profound meaning and fulfillment in our own. It is never too late to pick up the pen and write the chapters of our lives.

Seniors choosing not to chronicle their entire lives can still derive immense value from writing a book focused on distilled lessons, learned mistakes, and acquired skill sets. This approach offers a concentrated exploration of personal growth and experiences, providing readers with practical insights and guidance. For instance, they might share life lessons, turning points, and the wisdom gained, serving as a roadmap for navigating the complexities of life. Our seniors can opt for more specialized approaches - crafting books that share expertise in a specific field or passion cultivated over the years, be it gardening tips, financial wisdom, or anecdotes blending humor with valuable insights. The act of writing becomes a means of self-reflection and a legacy of accumulated wisdom, offering a purposeful and enriching contribution to the collective knowledge of generations.

Here are some ideas, you may want to explore if you aren't ready to write a memoir or autobiography…

Life Lessons and Wisdom:

Share accumulated wisdom and life lessons, offering guidance to future generations.

Expertise and Guides:

Compile expertise in a specific field, creating a guide or manual on topics mastered over the years.

Anecdotal Collections:

Create a collection of anecdotes, humor, and reflections, providing a lighthearted yet insightful read.

Passion Projects:

Focus on a particular passion, whether it's art, music, travel, or any area that has brought you joy and fulfillment.

Historical Accounts:

Document historical accounts or personal experiences that provide unique perspectives on certain periods.

Family History:

Write a comprehensive family history, preserving genealogy, traditions, and shared memories.

Legacy Letters:

Compose letters to family members, offering personal insights, advice, and reflections.

Fictional Narratives:

Venture into fiction, crafting stories inspired by personal experiences or creative imagination.

Collaborative Writing:

Collaborate with others, engaging in joint projects that capture diverse perspectives and voices.

Poetry and Creative Writing:

Express thoughts and emotions through poetry or other creative writing forms.

Photography and Captioning:

Combine photographs with thoughtful captions, creating a visually engaging narrative.

Travelogues:

Document travel experiences, sharing adventures, cultural encounters, and personal reflections.

Recipes and Culinary Tales:

Compile favorite recipes along with culinary anecdotes, creating a personalized cookbook.

You can choose a combination of these approaches or focus on one that resonates most with your interests and objectives. Writing a book as a senior is a versatile and rewarding endeavor.

The Art of Growing Old

Become an entrepreneur

It's common for people to ease into retirement after lengthy careers, relishing the freedom from demanding schedules and routines. However, the mere idea of idleness, for me was unsettling. Additionally, as we've observed in preceding chapters, maintaining financial stability is crucial. I opted for consultancy work and assumed the role of brand ambassador for iFranchise. This was one of the wisest decisions I made. My role as the brand ambassador and consultant allows me flexibility of time and gives me the opportunity to travel, meet new people, and use my skills and experience.

Well-researched entrepreneurship is a path seniors can choose, which not only fills time but offers a source of renewed purpose. By starting a business, retirees can supplement their retirement income, achieving peace of mind as well as maintaining their desired standard of living. Entrepreneurship in retirement offers a level of flexibility and autonomy. Being your own boss means setting your own schedule, choosing the projects you work on, and deciding how much time to devote to your business.

Whether it's spending more time with family, pursuing hobbies, or traveling, entrepreneurship provides the freedom to structure one's life according to personal needs and interests.

It also fosters continuous learning, because starting a business calls for acquiring new skills, adapting to changing market dynamics, and being well informed and alert to overcome challenges. This ongoing process of learning keeps the mind sharp and stimulated, promoting cognitive health and well-being.

Entrepreneurship, therefore, also helps one stay intellectually engaged well into their later years. And this can be our last attempt at leaving a legacy and making a positive impact on future generations. Building a successful business is creating something meaningful that transcends one's lifetime.

Seniors can pass down their knowledge, values, and

experiences to future generations, inspiring others to pursue their dreams and make a difference in the world.

However, a word of caution – one should be extremely careful and weigh the pros and cons, and assess the risks involved before diving in. We don't want to lose our hard-earned money from years of labor going down the drain.

Here are some key steps to consider when assessing the viability of an entrepreneurial endeavor…

Market Research:

Conduct thorough market research to understand the demand for your product or service. Identify your target audience, their needs, and preferences. Analyze market trends, competitor offerings, and potential gaps in the market that your idea can address.

Financial Feasibility:

Evaluate the financial viability of your business idea. Estimate startup costs, ongoing expenses, and projected revenue. Create a detailed financial plan, including cash flow projections and break-even analysis. Consider how your retirement savings and other financial resources will be allocated to support the business.

Risk Assessment:

Identify and assess potential risks associated with your entrepreneurial venture. Consider both external factors, such as economic conditions and regulatory changes, and internal factors, such as operational challenges and resource limitations. Develop contingency plans to
mitigate risks and adapt to unforeseen circumstances.

Professional Advice:

Seek guidance from experienced mentors, business advisors, or industry experts. Their insights and expertise can provide valuable perspective and help you navigate potential pitfalls. Also, consult lawyers to ensure that your business complies with legal and regulatory requirements. Remember, our aim is to have a peaceful life.

Ensuring the safety and viability of a business idea is paramount for seniors venturing into entrepreneurship.
Here are some strategies to help you zero in on a business idea with confidence:

Reflect on Your Interests and Passions:

Start by considering your interests, hobbies, and passions accumulated over a lifetime. Think about activities that bring you joy, fulfillment, and a sense of purpose. Whether it's gardening, cooking, crafting, or mentoring others, exploring your passions can spark ideas for a business that resonates with your values and interests.

Draw from Your Professional Experience:

Leverage your professional experience and expertise gained throughout your career. Reflect on your skills, knowledge, and strengths that can be applied to entrepreneurial endeavors. Identify industry trends, emerging opportunities, or unmet needs that align with your expertise and experience. Your unique insights and perspective can inspire innovative business ideas tailored to your niche market.

Identify Market Gaps and Opportunities:

Observe your surroundings and identify gaps or inefficiencies in the market that present opportunities for innovation. Pay attention to consumer needs, trends, and emerging technologies that can shape new business opportunities. Conduct market research, gather feedback from potential customers and analyze competitor offerings to identify areas where you can differentiate and add value.

Solve Problems and Address Pain Points:

Think about challenges or frustrations you've encountered personally or observed in your community. Developing solutions that alleviate pain points and improve people's lives can form the basis of a compelling business proposition.

Explore Franchise or Licensing opportunities:

For retirees seeking a turnkey business opportunity with established brand recognition and support, exploring franchise or licensing opportunities can be an attractive option. Research franchise concepts or licensing agreements that align with your interests, values, and financial resources. Evaluate the track record, reputation, and support services offered by franchisors or licensors to ensure a good fit for your entrepreneurial goals.

Prioritize selecting a business idea that harmonizes with your desired lifestyle. Carefully assess the time and effort demanded by the venture, ensuring it doesn't encroach excessively on your well-deserved leisure time.

After decades of dedication and hard work, it's essential to avoid unnecessary stress and strain. By choosing an idea that allows for a manageable workload and a fulfilling retirement, you can embark on your entrepreneurial journey with confidence and enjoyment.

The Art of Growing Old

Earn in your PJs

For retirees seeking financial freedom in their later years while also cherishing the comfort of home and leisure time, starting an online business presents an appealing option. No more ties, blazers, or 8 am schedules - just the simple pleasure of sipping morning coffee in peace and relishing favorite meals at an elegantly laid out dining table with family, all while earning some extra cash from the convenience of home.

However, the hurdle for many seniors, especially those post-60 years, is the reluctance to embrace technology. Understandably so, because we did not grow up with computers and smartphones; we come from an era when postcards were the norm, and the advent of phone calls and mobiles was groundbreaking enough, let alone the concept of artificial intelligence (AI).

Here's my sincere suggestion: start by learning basic technology skills. Let's not dive into AI just yet if you're not comfortable. Focus on mastering simple online basics to kickstart an online business. With these skills, you can earn easy money sitting at home in your PJs, enjoying the freedom and flexibility that comes with being your own boss in the digital world. E-commerce platforms and digital marketplaces not only offer us a global audience for our products or services, but also foster a sense of purpose and engagement, helping us stay active, mentally stimulated, and socially connected.

Since COVID-19, many older folks have realized they can make money online. With lockdowns, they couldn't do their usual jobs, so they tried something new. For example, there's Richard Thompson, a former accountant who launched a virtual financial consulting business, and Maria Garcia, a retired teacher who began selling homemade baked goods online. These seniors show how anyone can use the internet to start a business, even after retirement.

Here are some types of online businesses seniors may consider:

Drop shipping:

With drop shipping, seniors can create an online store to sell products without the need to hold inventory. Instead, when a customer makes a purchase, the product is shipped directly from the supplier to the customer. This eliminates the need for storage space and upfront investment in inventory, making it an attractive option for retirees looking to start an e-commerce business with minimal risk.

Print-on-Demand:

Print-on-demand allows seniors to design and sell custom products such as T-shirts, mugs, and phone cases without the need for inventory or production equipment. When a customer places an order, the product is printed and shipped directly from the printing company. This business model offers low overhead costs and the flexibility to create unique, personalized items tailored to specific niches or interests.

Affiliate Marketing:

Affiliate marketing is a convenient source of income. It is a partnership with companies where we promote products or services through our online platforms, such as websites, blogs, or social media. When our audience makes a purchase through a special link provided by us, we earn a commission on the sale. It's a win-win situation: we get paid for promoting products we believe in, and companies gain exposure to a new audience.

The options are numerous: skincare partnerships, fashion and apparel partnerships, fitness brand partnerships, home and lifestyle sponsorships are the most commonly seen affiliations that seniors opt for.

For retirees seeking to curate a personalized shopping experience, the e-commerce landscape beckons with its promise of autonomy and creativity. Establishing an online store enables retirees to showcase their craftsmanship or curate niche products to a global audience.

However, like any entrepreneurial endeavor, it's essential to recognize and address potential risks that may arise along the way. Most common challenges include:

Technological Challenges:

From setting up websites and navigating social media platforms to understanding digital marketing tools, the learning curve can be steep. Moreover, technological advancements evolve rapidly, requiring retirees to stay abreast of new trends and updates, which may pose a challenge.

Financial Investment:

Launching and maintaining an online marketing business often entails financial investments, such as website hosting fees, marketing expenses and purchasing inventory. So, allocate resources prudently to mitigate the risk of overspending.

Market Volatility:

The digital marketplace is dynamic and subject to fluctuations influenced by factors such as consumer trends, economic conditions, and technological innovations. Be prepared to adapt to changing market dynamics and consumer preferences.

Cybersecurity Threats:

Cybersecurity threats such as phishing frauds, malware attacks, and data breaches can pose challenges. These risks can compromise sensitive information, including personal and financial data, posing significant threats to retirees' financial security and online reputation.

Regulatory Compliance:

Navigating the regulatory landscape of online marketing requires adhering to legal guidelines and industry regulations governing areas such as consumer protection, data privacy, and advertising standards. Failure to comply with relevant regulations can result in legal consequences, damage to your reputation, and financial penalties. Stay well informed.

Health and Well-being:

Long hours spent in front of screens, managing deadlines, and handling customer inquiries may exacerbate existing health conditions or lead to stress-related ailments if not managed effectively.

Despite the risks and challenges that come with launching an online business during retirement, the rewards and opportunities far outweigh the potential drawbacks. In every aspect of life, whether personal or professional, risks exist, but it's often the willingness to step outside our comfort zones and embrace new possibilities that leads to growth and fulfillment. The same holds true for seniors venturing into online entrepreneurship.

So, let's look at the brighter side. Online entrepreneurship allows retirees to enjoy the best of both worlds: spending quality time with loved ones while pursuing entrepreneurial passions and securing their financial future beyond social security income. Imagine hosting family gatherings, playing with grandchildren, or indulging in an afternoon nap, all while managing a thriving online business.

Online entrepreneurship is the most convenient way to supplement retirement income in the face of rising living costs and unforeseen expenses.

Also, the potential for scalability and growth inherent in online business models means that retirees have the opportunity to build sustainable revenue streams that can support them well into their golden years.

The Art of Growing Old

Become a silver influencer

Seniors are uniquely positioned to become powerful voices in today's digital landscape. Have you given this a thought?

The digital era has given rise to armchair experts. Anyone with a smartphone and the gift of the gab is an expert. Social influencers are increasingly shaping trends, opinions, and consumer behavior across various platforms. They possess a significant following on social media platforms such as Instagram, YouTube, LinkedIn, Facebook, or TikTok and cover everything from product endorsements and lifestyle tips to personal anecdotes. This is where we seniors can play a powerful role.

With the immense experience we have garnered over decades, both professional and personal, why not share our knowledge and experience. Let's become 'silver' influencers!

Sandra Hart, a YouTube influencer, writes on her channel 'Life with Sandra Hart': "I am 85 and I share intimate chats about life. I'm here to dispel the fear of aging and to help us all navigate life, no matter how old or young you are. This is our time to shine and it is an amazing adventure we are all on."

Old Man Steve is also an octogenarian influencer with huge followers on YouTube, Instagram and TikTok. He writes, "I'm 85 years old and just having some fun doing my thing. I tell stories and have fun with calls on my banana phone. I do some cooking and a little dancing now and then."

At 93 years old, Baddie Winkle has gained a massive following on Instagram (@baddiewinkle) by showcasing her bold fashion choices and carefree attitude. She challenges age stereotypes and inspires her followers to embrace self-expression and confidence.

Grandma Joy on TikTok (@grandma_joy), is 88 years old. She shares heartwarming videos of her daily life, offering words of wisdom and spreading positivity to her audience. Her infectious smile and uplifting messages have garnered her a loyal following.

These seniors have demonstrated that age is no barrier to building a substantial following and making an impact with their content. Through their expertise, humor, and authenticity, they have captured the hearts and minds of millions of viewers around the globe.

Here are some reasons why we can become great silver influencers:

Generosity:

Many seniors have a strong sense of generosity and a desire to give back. As silver influencers, we can use this platform to promote causes we care about and encourage others to get involved.

Life Experience:

Seniors have lived through a wide range of experiences, including triumphs, challenges, and everything in between. This wealth of life experience gives us a unique perspective that will resonate with people.

Wisdom:

With age often comes wisdom. Seniors have had the

opportunity to learn from their successes and failures, offering valuable insights and advice to others.

Authenticity:

Seniors are typically unapologetically themselves. We are not trying to impress anyone or fit into a particular mold. This authenticity is refreshing and fosters genuine connections with their audience.

Relatability:

Many of the experience's seniors have gone through are universal. Whether it's raising a family, pursuing a career, or enjoying hobbies, our stories and insights can resonate with people of all ages.

Adaptability:

Seniors have shown resilience and adaptability throughout their lives, navigating various changes and challenges. This adaptability extends to social media, where they can learn and grow alongside younger generations.

Role Models:

Seniors can serve as positive role models for individuals of all ages. By showcasing our active lifestyles, pursuing passions, and staying engaged in our communities, we inspire others to embrace aging with grace and enthusiasm.

Storytelling:

Seniors are often natural storytellers. Whether recounting memories from our youth or sharing anecdotes from recent adventures, we have a knack for captivating the audience and leaving a lasting impression.

Respect:

Seniors often command respect and admiration from younger generations due to our life experiences and wisdom. We can help bridge generational gaps and foster mutual understanding and appreciation.

Now, let's explore step by step how seniors can leverage their wisdom, authenticity, and passion to become influential voices in the realm of social media…

Identify Your Passion:

Start by identifying your interests and passions. Whether it's gardening, cooking, travel, literature, or any other hobby or topic you're passionate about, choosing a niche that you genuinely enjoy will make the process more enjoyable and sustainable.

Choose Your Platform:

Decide which social media platform(s) align best with your interests and target audience. Options include Facebook, Instagram, YouTube, TikTok, and blogging platforms like WordPress or Medium. Consider where your potential audience spends their time, and which platform best suits your content style.

Create a Profile:

Set up a profile on your chosen social media platform(s). Use a clear profile picture and write a compelling bio that highlights who you are, what you're passionate about, and what your audience can expect from your content.

Develop Your Content Strategy:

Define the type of content you want to create and how often you'll post. This could include sharing personal stories, offering tips and advice, creating tutorials, or showcasing your creations or experiences. Tailor your content to resonate with your target audience while staying true to your authentic voice.

Start Creating Content:

Begin creating and sharing content on a regular basis. Consistency is key to building a following on social media. Establish a regular posting schedule and stick to it. This could be daily, weekly, or whatever frequency works best for you. Experiment with different formats, such as photos, videos, captions, and blog posts, to see what resonates best with your audience. Focus on providing value and engaging with your followers through comments, likes, and shares.

Engage with Your Audience:

Actively engage with your audience by responding to comments, asking questions, and participating in conversations. Building genuine connections with your followers will help foster a loyal and supportive community around your content.

Collaborate and Network:

Collaborate with other influencers or creators in your niche to expand your reach and connect with new audiences. Networking with like-minded individuals can also provide valuable support, advice, and opportunities for growth.

Stay Consistent and Persistent:

Building a social media presence takes time and consistency. Stay committed to your content schedule and continue refining your strategy based on feedback and analytics. Be patient and persistent, knowing that growth may take time but that every effort contributes to your progress.

Monitor and Adapt:

Monitor your analytics regularly to track your progress and identify areas for improvement. Pay attention to which types of content perform best and adjust your strategy accordingly. Stay informed about trends and changes in your niche or platform to stay relevant and continue growing your influence.

Stay Authentic:

Remain true to yourself and your values as you grow your influence on social media. Authenticity is what sets you apart and builds trust with your audience.

While the benefits are many, there are also risks that retirees should be aware of. One potential risk is the exposure to online criticism and negativity. On social media, not everyone will be supportive, and some people may leave hurtful comments or try to undermine your efforts.

Additionally, seniors may encounter challenges with technology and online privacy. It's important to take precautions to protect personal information and stay vigilant against frauds or cyber threats. Seniors should also be mindful of the time and energy required to maintain a social media presence, as it can be demanding and potentially overwhelming.

To mitigate these risks, we can take several precautionary measures. Firstly, let's aptly educate ourselves about online safety and privacy best practices. This includes using strong passwords, being cautious about sharing personal information, and being selective about the content we engage with. It's also helpful to establish boundaries and take breaks when needed to avoid burnout. By being proactive and taking steps to protect ourselves, we can confidently embrace social media as a platform for becoming influencers while minimizing potential pitfalls.

The Art of Growing Old

Start an NGO

Have you thought of setting up an NGO? It's one of the best ways to give back to your community and people. Through non-governmental organizations (NGOs), seniors can not only effectively and productively channel their time but also put their skills to great use Here are some reasons you may consider to set up an NGO:

Experience and Expertise:

I can never stress enough about experience. As mentioned in previous chapters, our wealth of experience and expertise is a treasure. Whether you were teachers, doctors, engineers, or business leaders, retirees have valuable skills and knowledge that can be harnessed to address social, environmental, or humanitarian issues through NGOs.

Purpose and Meaning:

The vacuum one feels from having no routine, which may

trigger a sense of loss of purpose and identity, can be overcome by starting an NGO. And this is a gift to the future generations, too.

Community Engagement:

Most of us have extensive networks and connections built over a lifetime. By starting NGOs, we can leverage our community ties to mobilize resources, raise awareness about important issues, and foster collaboration among stakeholders to drive positive change at the grassroots level.

Health and Well-being:

Numerous studies have shown that staying socially engaged and mentally stimulated in old age contributes to better health and well-being. Consider starting an NGO to help others lead a healthy, high-quality life.

Continued Learning and Growth:

Starting an NGO presents seniors with opportunities to learn new skills, tackle complex challenges, master fundraising techniques, navigate legal regulations, or hone leadership abilities.

There are numerous individuals who have started NGOs after retirement. For instance, Paul Newman, the legendary actor, founded Newman's Own Foundation after retiring from acting.

The foundation is known for its philanthropic efforts, including funding initiatives related to children's health, education, and environmental conservation. Jimmy Carter, former U.S. President, started the Carter Center after leaving Office. The organization works to advance human rights, promote democracy, and improve global health, with initiatives ranging from conflict resolution to disease eradication. Kiran Bedi, the first woman to join the Indian Police Service, founded the Navjyoti India Foundation after retiring from the police force.

The NGO focuses on social and community development, with programs addressing issues such as education, healthcare, and women's empowerment. The examples around us are many…

So, how do we get started? Let's look into the steps and challenges:

Identify a Cause:

Seniors should first identify a cause or issue they care deeply about. This could be anything from environmental conservation to providing education for underprivileged children.

Conduct Research:

Once you have chosen a cause, research existing NGOs working in that field to understand what gaps exist and how you can contribute effectively.

Build a Team:

Starting an NGO often requires teamwork. Seniors can reach out to like-minded individuals, community members, or professionals who share their passion and are willing to collaborate.

Develop a Mission and Vision:

Clearly define the mission and vision of your NGO, outlining its goals, objectives, and the impact you hope to achieve.

Register the NGO:

Depending on the country and legal requirements, you may need to register the NGO with the appropriate authorities.

This typically involves completing paperwork and fulfilling certain criteria.

Fundraising and Resource Mobilization:

Explore various avenues for fundraising, such as seeking donations, organizing events, or applying for grants. You can also leverage your networks and connections to mobilize resources.

Implement Programs and Projects:

With the necessary resources in place, you may start implementing programs and projects to address the identified issue. This may involve partnering with other organizations, conducting outreach activities, or providing direct services.

Monitor and Evaluate:

It's essential for seniors to monitor the progress of their NGO's activities and evaluate their impact regularly. This helps ensure that resources are used effectively and that the organization remains accountable to its stakeholders.

There are many types of NGOs you may consider:

Community Development NGOs:

These NGOs focus on improving the well-being of communities by addressing issues such as poverty, healthcare, education, and infrastructure development.

Environmental NGOs:

Those passionate about environmental conservation can start NGOs dedicated to protecting natural resources, promoting sustainability, and raising awareness about environmental issues.

Senior Citizen NGOs:

NGOs that cater specifically to the needs and interests of older adults, providing support services, advocacy, and social activities for seniors in their communities.

Education NGOs:

NGOs focused on education can provide learning opportunities, scholarships, and resources to underprivileged children, adults, or specific groups within the community.

Arts and Culture NGOs:

Seniors with a passion for arts and culture can start NGOs

that promote artistic expression, preserve cultural heritage, and provide opportunities for artistic development and appreciation.

As with any venture, NGOs, too, need meticulous monitoring to be successful. For instance, Kids Company, was a charity providing support to vulnerable children and young people in the UK, which shut down in 2015 following financial mismanagement and governance issues. One Laptop per Child (OLPC), set up to provide affordable laptops to children in developing countries to improve education, faced criticism for its implementation and sustainability challenges, including issues with content delivery and teacher training. You will find many such examples.

Below are some of the challenges you may face in setting up NGOs:

Limited Resources:

One of the main challenges is limited financial resources to fund NGO activities.

Lack of Technical Skills:

Lack of technical skills, such as computer literacy or

knowledge of legal regulations, required to establish and operate an NGO is the most commonly seen challenge.

Navigating Bureaucracy:

Dealing with bureaucratic procedures and paperwork involved in registering an NGO can be daunting for seniors.

Building a Supportive Network:

Seniors may struggle to build a supportive network of volunteers, donors, and community partners to sustain their NGO's activities.

Sustainability:

Ensuring long-term sustainability of the NGO beyond their own involvement can also be challenging. But take heart! There is no challenge that does not have a solution. To get money, you can ask for donations, apply for grants, or host events in communities to raise funds.

If you are not sure how to do certain things, like using computers or understanding legal stuff, ask younger volunteers or professionals for help. When it comes to paperwork and rules for starting an NGO, you can get help from legal experts or groups that know about this stuff. And what are friends and family for? Seek their help.

Be creative

Creativity is a misunderstood word. When we say an individual is creative, the most common notion is they are into the Arts. While that is by far correct, thinking outside the box, breaking free from conventional patterns, and embracing experimentation and innovation is also creativity. Our ability to generate new ideas, solutions, or expressions that are original and meaningful is creativity.

The truth is that creativity knows no age limits. As we grow older, embracing creativity becomes not only a means of self-expression but also a pathway to continued growth, fulfillment, and well-being. In fact, I believe seniors must embrace creativity because it helps us stay healthy.

Brain Development:
Engaging in creative activities stimulates neural pathways in the brain, promoting cognitive function and mental agility.

Research has shown that seniors who participate in creative pursuits may experience improved memory, concentration, and problem-solving skills.

Psychological Well-being:

Creativity serves as a powerful outlet for self-expression and emotional release, contributing to enhanced mood, reduced stress, and increased feelings of happiness and fulfillment. Creative activities provide seniors with a sense of purpose, identity, and accomplishment, fostering a positive outlook on life.

Physiological Health:

Creativity has been linked to physiological benefits, such as reduced risk of cognitive decline, lower blood pressure, and improved immune function. Engaging in creative pursuits promotes relaxation, mindfulness, and overall physical well-being.

So, by embracing creativity in their senior years, individuals can stimulate their minds, nurture their spirits, and foster a sense of purpose and fulfillment. Whether through visual arts, writing, music, crafts, or culinary endeavors, seniors have a wealth of creative pursuits to explore, each offering unique opportunities for self-expression, growth, and joy.

Here are some examples of people being creatively strange:

The Pencil Tip Sculptor:

Artist Dalton Ghetti, a sexagenarian, creates intricate sculptures out of pencil tips. Using only a razor blade and a sewing needle, he meticulously carves tiny sculptures, such as animals, people, and objects, directly into the graphite of pencils.

The Human Statue:

Performance artist Johan Lorbeer, a septuagenarian, is known for his gravity-defying stunts where he appears to be floating or defying gravity while leaning against walls or perched on buildings. Through the clever use of hidden supports and strategic body positioning, he creates surreal and captivating visual illusions.

Grandma Moses (Anna Mary Robertson Moses):

Grandma Moses began painting in her late 70s and gained widespread recognition for her folk art depicting rural life in America. Despite starting late in life, her artistic talent and unique style made her one of the most celebrated American artists of the 20th century.

The Junk Artist:

Sculptor Dan Tague, a quinquagenarian, creates thought-provoking artworks using everyday objects and materials found in junkyards and thrift stores. His sculptures often convey social or political messages, such as consumerism, environmentalism, and societal norms, through the juxtaposition and manipulation of found objects.

Frank Gehry:

Renowned architect Frank Gehry continued to push the boundaries of architectural design well into his senior years. His iconic buildings, characterized by bold and innovative forms, have left an indelible mark on the world of architecture.

Mary Oliver:

Pulitzer Prize-winning poet Mary Oliver, who found acclaim for her profound and contemplative verses, wrote until her last days.

Let's not slow down in our later years, and instead embrace the opportunity to explore various artistic endeavors – from painting and sculpture to writing and music, we can find fulfillment, joy, and purpose in our creative endeavors.

Here are some pursuits you may consider:

Visual Arts:

Painting: Whether it's watercolors, acrylics, oils, or pastels, painting offers seniors a means of self-expression and exploration of color and form.

Drawing: From sketching to doodling, drawing allows seniors to capture the world around them and unleash their imagination.

Sculpture: Working with clay, wood, or other materials enables seniors to create three-dimensional artworks and enjoy tactile experiences.

Crafting:

Knitting and Crocheting: These timeless crafts not only produce cozy garments and accessories but also provide a sense of relaxation and accomplishment.

Sewing and Quilting: Seniors can create beautiful clothing, home décor, and intricate quilts while honing their sewing skills.

Pottery and Ceramics: Getting hands-on with clay allows seniors to shape functional or decorative objects and embrace the therapeutic nature of pottery.

Performing Arts:

Music: Learning to play an instrument or joining a choir offers seniors opportunities for self-expression, social interaction, and cognitive stimulation.

Theater: Seniors can participate in community theater productions, storytelling, or improv workshops to explore their dramatic talents and connect with others.

Dance: Whether it's ballroom, line dancing, or contemporary styles, dancing promotes physical fitness, coordination, and emotional well-being.

Writing and Literature:

Memoir Writing: Documenting life experiences and memories through writing allows seniors to leave a legacy for future generations and reflect on their journey.

Poetry: Crafting poetry provides a creative outlet for expressing emotions, thoughts, and observations in a concise and impactful manner.

Book Clubs: Joining or forming a book club fosters

intellectual stimulation, social connections, and lively discussions about literature.

Digital Arts:

Photography: Seniors can explore the world through the lens of a camera, capturing moments, landscapes, and portraits to share with others.

Graphic Design: Using digital tools and software, seniors can unleash their creativity in designing logos, posters, digital illustrations, and more.

Video Editing: Creating and editing videos allows seniors to tell stories, preserve memories, and share their experiences with others in dynamic ways.

Cooking and Culinary Arts:

Exploring new recipes, experimenting with ingredients, and sharing meals with loved ones can be a deliciously creative way for seniors to express their culinary talents.

Birdwatching and Nature Observation:

Spending time in Nature is therapeutic. Step outdoors observing birds, wildlife, and natural landscapes. Keeping a nature journal or sketchbook and document observations, thoughts, and reflections. Later you can share it with enthusiasts or even consider publishing it as a book, or contributing your learnings to universities, schools and libraries.

DIY Home Projects:

Seniors are the best people to help around the house. Volunteer for DIY (do-it-yourself) home improvement projects, such as painting walls, refurbishing furniture, or redecorating rooms. Repurposing old items into something new and functional can spark creativity and provide a sense of accomplishment.

Gardening:

Seniors can cultivate a garden, whether it's a small plot in their backyard, a community garden plot, or even indoor plants. Experimenting with different plants, flowers, and landscaping techniques allows seniors to express themselves creatively while enjoying the beauty of nature.

So, being creative as we get older is super important! It's not just about making cool stuff, it's about feeling good, too. Being creative helps us stay sharp, happy, and connected. Try new things, have fun, and keep those creative juices flowing. You'll be amazed at how much joy and fulfillment it can bring to your life.

MINDFUL MUSINGS

Reflect on how gardening or nurturing plants can reignite a sense of purpose and joy in your life. How do you feel when you connect with nature?

_____

_____

_____

_____

What new skills or hobbies related to gardening would you like to explore, and how can they enhance your daily life?

_____

_____

_____

How do you redefine your role and identity in your home as you age? What activities make you feel like a star in your own house?

What home projects or domestic skills have you always wanted to master, and how can you start incorporating them into your routine?

The Art of Growing Old

_____

_____

_____

_____

What steps can you take to reinvent yourself or pursue a new passion as you age? Reflect on any past experiences where you successfully reinvented yourself.

_____

_____

_____

_____

_____

How can embracing change and new experiences contribute to your personal growth and happiness?

How do you stay connected and engaged in the digital age? What technology or online platforms have enhanced your life?

Reflect on any challenges you face with technology. How can you overcome these challenges to stay connected and informed?

_____

_____

_____

_____

How can writing or journaling serve as a creative outlet and a way to process your experiences? What topics are you passionate about writing?

_____

_____

_____

Reflect on any writing projects you've started or wish to start. How can you use writing to leave a legacy or share your wisdom with others?

What business ideas have you always wanted to explore? Reflect on how starting your own business could bring fulfillment and purpose to your life.

_____

_____

_____

_____

What steps can you take to turn your entrepreneurial dreams into reality? How can your past experiences and skills support your new venture?

_____

_____

_____

_____

_____

How do you envision working from home or starting a

home-based business? What kind of work-from-home opportunities align with your skills and interests?

_____

_____

_____

_____

Reflect on the benefits and challenges of working from home. How can you create a productive and satisfying work environment in your own space?

_____

_____

_____

_____

What unique perspectives and experiences can you share as a silver influencer? How can you use social media to inspire and connect with others?

_____

_____

_____

_____

Reflect on the impact you want to have as an influencer. How can you use your platform to promote positive change and support your community?

_____

_____

What causes or issues are you passionate about? Reflect on how starting an NGO could help you address these issues and make a difference.

What skills and resources do you need to start and run an NGO? How can you begin taking steps toward this goal?

The Art of Growing Old

_____

_____

_____

_____

How do you currently express your creativity, and what new creative activities would you like to try? Reflect on the role of creativity in your life.

_____

_____

_____

_____

_____

What benefits do you experience from engaging in creative pursuits? How can you incorporate more creativity into your daily routine?

_____

_____

_____

_____

_____

SECTION: IV

Growing Old the Gen X, Millennial & Gen Z way

Without remorse or regret rearing ahead

The Art of Growing Old

As I reflect on my own journey of aging, I recognize the value of seeking diverse perspectives on this universal experience. While my own insights as a 62-year-old offer a firsthand account of navigating the later years, I believe it's equally crucial to understand how younger generations perceive the concept of growing old.

Therefore, I'm excited to include a Gen X, Millennial and Gen Z perspective in this book. Timothy St Louis [my younger son] helped me fetch valuable insights from the younger lot's evolving attitudes, expectations, and challenges surrounding aging in today's society.

Hope this intergenerational point of view will help you foster a wholesome understanding of the art of growing old.

*The young say –
Growing old is having lived a
life on your own terms.*

As I journey through the exploration of growing old, I find myself drawn to various perspectives, each offering a unique lens through which to view the aging process. Timothy St. Louis, a vibrant 36-year-old artist and CEO, known in creative circles as Indy Nyles, challenges the conventional narrative of aging, urging us to rethink the predefined milestones of success and fulfillment.

Timothy candidly reflects on his journey of breaking free from societal expectations and embracing authenticity, transcending the traditional 'American dream' narrative. Raised amidst pervasive pressure to achieve financial milestones and conform to predetermined life trajectories, Timothy expresses disillusionment with this path. He advocates carving out one's unique journey, liberated from societal norms.

For Timothy, growing old goes beyond reaching a certain age or meeting societal expectations. It's about living on his terms, pursuing passions, and prioritizing personal fulfillment. His narrative underscores the courage to defy expectations and forge a unique path aligned with one's desires and aspirations.

Success, to Timothy, extends beyond monetary gains and societal validation. He shares his struggle to reconcile societal expectations with his innermost desires, refusing to succumb to the societal mold. Instead, Timothy embraces his identity as an artist and entrepreneur, finding fulfillment in authenticity and purpose.

He left behind a career in retail management to embark on a journey of self-discovery and reinvention. Through perseverance and self-belief, he discovered a newfound sense of purpose, marking his departure from traditional notions of success.

Craig Gonzalez, a 46-year-old web developer from Detroit,

also emphasizes the importance of balancing work and leisure. Gonzalez is passionate about curling, DJing, and camping, and vouches how these activities contribute to his personal fulfillment. However, he doesn't solely rely on his art for income to diminish its enjoyment, emphasizing the importance of maintaining a separation between his passion and his job. Craig appreciates his current situation, where he pursues his artistic endeavors alongside a stable 9 to 5 job without financial strain.

Optimistic about personal growth, Craig encourages embracing change and seizing new opportunities without succumbing to societal expectations. Transitioning into web development in his 30s, he emphasizes adaptability and lifelong learning, advocating for a proactive approach to life.

However, even as he values ambition, he is uncertain about future plans, being content in his current living situation, enjoying his neighborhood and house since purchasing it in 2020. He loves traveling and gets excited about the unknown but is cautious about making long-term plans, preferring to embrace spontaneity and adaptability.

Meanwhile, 35-year-old Ere Lo, is concerned about the

prevalence of body dysmorphia among people of her age, particularly focusing on the challenges women face regarding economic independence in Latin America. She is disturbed by the significant gender disparity in economic opportunities, leading many women to seek financial support from men to improve their lives.

A staunch advocate for equal pay between genders to alleviate such struggles, Ere is skeptical about the possibility of meaningful change because of the deep-rooted patriarchy that is still prevalent across cultures and industries.

Ere firmly believes in the power of empathy and communal sharing to foster strong communities and partnerships, especially as individuals age. She has observed that those who prioritize these values tend to encounter fewer challenges in their later years. Ere offers examples of people who choose to live communally with friends, sharing responsibilities and meals.

She highlights how such arrangements significantly contribute to overall happiness and well-being. Ere volunteers in a community and is currently co-authoring a book, too. She had a clothing store, which she had to shut down during the pandemic and is into home décor now, helping clients settle into their new homes.

A stable home results in emotionally-stable children. 45-year-old Maurice Franklin from Michigan calls himself a happy person. He says that he was aware early in childhood that he was blessed to be raised by both mom and dad. And he always knew he wanted to be the best possible person growing up, even when no one is perfect.

At the age of around 28, Maurice began to take life more seriously, realizing his purpose was to assist people and give back to youth. He believes in self-drive and maintaining faith, asserting that as long as he spreads positivity, it will eventually return to him. Maurice stresses that blessings may not arrive immediately, but he trusts in a higher plan and readiness to receive them.

Despite challenges, Maurice emphasizes that one doesn't need to be wealthy to make a difference. Whether it's providing meals or school supplies, he demonstrates care for his community, aiming to show young individuals that they are valued. Maurice believes in instilling respect and adaptability in social interactions, advocating for traditional values while adapting to various settings without compromising authenticity.

He compares adaptability to a chameleon, essential for navigating life's diverse situations successfully. Maurice draws from his experiences working with adolescents, emphasizing the importance of teaching these skills early on for future success. He encourages individuals not to limit themselves to one goal or occupation, stressing the importance of versatility in life's journey. He insists on having more than one goal in life. 'You are more than just one occupation.'

Meg Juma, 31-year-old career coach, specializes in working with women. With four years of experience running her coaching business, she embraces entering her 30s with a sense of confidence and fulfillment. Reflecting on her journey, Meg acknowledges that maturity unfolds uniquely for each individual and regrets not fully embracing her path sooner. She wished she had possessed the confidence to pursue her goals without comparing herself to others her age, recognizing that earlier commitment to her own path could have led to greater achievements without conforming to societal expectations.

Despite having a sense of her aspirations at 18, Meg didn't fully commit to her chosen path until age 25, attributing this delay to societal pressures and comparison with peers. During those years, she felt unfulfilled as she lived according to expectations rather than following her true desires.

Looking ahead, Meg envisions pushing the boundaries of her abilities and expanding her business globally, particularly focusing on consultancy around NGOs and women's economic empowerment. To achieve these goals, she emphasizes the importance of planting seeds now and investing in networking, product quality, and personal development. Meg recognizes the need to reduce distractions, prioritize alone time, and focus on creating solutions, programs, and resources to empower women.

Meg advocates for adopting a beginner's mindset at every life stage and setting intentions to contribute meaningfully to each phase. She practices reassessing her priorities every five years to align with life's evolution, allowing her to embrace new seasons and reflect on the legacy or impact she aims to leave behind.

Similarly, Ugo Ememe, an engineer with nearly 20 years of experience in the energy industry, underscores the importance of intellectual engagement as retirement approaches, believing that mere relaxation isn't fulfilling. He stresses the need to keep the mind active to prevent cognitive decline. Ememe's perception of success has evolved, especially after attending pre-retirement workshops, which emphasized that retirement marks a transition rather than an end. While his job brought fulfillment, he recognizes that true fulfillment comes from within and isn't solely work-dependent.

Ememe also considers family responsibilities. He discusses how his perspective on maintaining lifestyle has evolved due to economic uncertainty, leading him to explore avenues for financial freedom. Family support has been crucial throughout his career, providing stability and opportunities. Supporting his family serves as a driving force for success, and he refrains from labeling experiences as regrets, understanding that different paths yield different outcomes.

Meanwhile, a group of Gen Zs we spoke to say they do not really think about old age or even retirement. Maya, 21-year-old, a Sri Lankan national, says she is teaching herself not to have many landmarks in her 20s. "It's a bit of a liminal space age, and one that's usually spent just figuring things out. But still by my 30s, I'd want a stable job that pays me well and allows me to have my own place, surrounded by friends and feeling safe in my life - the same applies to my 40s onwards."

Mansoor, 22-year-old, an Indonesian, says that he definitely aims to be jovial and surrounded by people in his old age. "We are all going apart, all my cousins are in different countries pursuing studies, so I hope we stay in touch and meet often as we age, too. But as of now, I am focused on trying out jobs. I foresee myself settled in my career in the next decade and hopefully start a family. At present I am not particularly concerned beyond that."

Similar sentiments are echoed by 25-year-old Rudradeb, an Indian national. "I definitely don't want to be shriveled up in bed. My grandparents are in their late 70s and still love going out, enjoying life, and traveling, so I'd love to be like them. However, I haven't really thought about how I'd plan to live my life four decades from now. One thing is certain: I want to make my parents proud."

Castillo, a 24-year-old based in the UK, says he wants to get the best education possible. "After graduation I took up a part-time job, but I aim to do my Master's from London School of Economics and settle in my career in the next 5 years. I haven't seriously thought about what I'd do in my 50s. Perhaps live in a beautiful home with a loving family."

Regarding career decisions, Ememe's words have value. He prioritizes job satisfaction over financial gain, driven by personal values and the desire for meaningful work. He cautions against comparing one's journey to others and advise against distractions and the fear of missing out. He stresses the importance of making decisions right rather than making the right decision and emphasize staying focused on chosen paths.

Ememe offers advice on consistency and perseverance, noting that actions necessary for success are easy to do but also easy to neglect. They highlight the importance of patience and the journey towards achievement, emphasizing personal growth over immediate results. That's an important piece of advice for the younger generation.

As Timothy says, break out of all societal norms, but understand that everything you see on TV or social media these days is not really made to benefit everybody. He wishes for more posts about personal happiness and life stories, especially from older individuals. He believes such sharing could positively influence younger generations to embrace themselves and make a positive impact on the world. Lastly, he urges everyone to care for the Earth, emphasizing its vital importance for humanity.

The Art of Growing Old

10 timeless truths I wish for the young

Reflecting on the diverse perspectives shared by individuals of younger generations, I find myself intrigued by the evolving perceptions of aging and life fulfillment.

Many voices echo the sentiment of challenging societal norms and embracing authenticity. They speak of carving out one's path, of refusing to conform to expectations imposed by society. This rebellion against the status quo resonates with a yearning for freedom and self-discovery reminiscent of youthful idealism.

There is a common thread of optimism and resilience woven through these narratives. They emphasize the importance of balance, of pursuing passions alongside responsibilities. The notion of holistic living emerges, where work and leisure harmonize to create a fulfilling existence. It's about embracing change, viewing age as an opportunity for personal growth rather than a barrier to exploration.

Inner peace and contribution to the community emerge as central themes. Wisdom, gained through experience, is seen as a valuable asset to be shared with younger generations. There's a call for mutual respect and learning between age groups, recognizing that wisdom knows no age limit.

The importance of embracing new experiences is underscored, regardless of age. It's about staying curious, open-minded, and actively seeking joy in life's moments. From exploring new hobbies to venturing into uncharted territories, there's a celebration of first experiences.

Legacy and giving back emerge as fundamental principles guiding one's journey. It's not just about personal fulfillment but about having a positive impact on the world. The notion of gratitude permeates these reflections by youngsters, a recognition of the blessings bestowed upon them and a desire to pay it forward.

However, it's crucial to acknowledge the diversity of viewpoints, too. While younger individuals may embrace notions of personal exploration and fulfillment, older generations might perceive these values as a departure from the traditional ethos they were raised with.

Indeed, some from older generations may argue that younger individuals prioritize individualism over community, and that the pursuit of personal happiness sometimes appears to come at the expense of traditional values like duty and sacrifice. This perceived shift in priorities can lead to tensions and misunderstandings between generations.

However, rather than viewing these differences as sources of conflict, we can approach them as opportunities for dialogue and mutual understanding. It's essential to recognize that societal norms evolve over time, and what may have been considered conventional in one era may no longer hold true today.

From the perspective of older generations, there are invaluable lessons to be learned. Throughout history, older individuals have embodied qualities such as resilience, discipline, sacrifice, and a strong sense of community. Their experiences have forged them into pillars of strength, capable of weathering life's storms with grace and determination.

One of the most significant lessons younger generations can glean from their elders is the value of resilience in the face of adversity. Older individuals have navigated through countless challenges, demonstrating the power of perseverance and the importance of maintaining a positive outlook, even in the darkest of times.

Additionally, older generations often exhibit a strong work ethic and discipline, instilled through years of hard work and dedication. They understand the importance of setting goals, staying focused, and putting in the effort required to achieve success. By observing these disciplined approaches, younger individuals can cultivate similar habits of diligence and perseverance in their own lives.

Older individuals of my generation tend to prioritize community and interpersonal connections, valuing relationships above material wealth or personal gain. They derive fulfillment from the bonds they share with family, friends, and neighbors, recognizing that true happiness often stems from meaningful connections with others. We demonstrate a profound sense of sacrifice and selflessness, putting the needs of their families and communities above their own. Whether it's working long hours to provide for loved ones or volunteering time to support those in need, older generations exemplify the spirit of altruism and compassion.

It's essential for both young and old to find a balance between tradition and innovation, honoring the past while also embracing the opportunities of the future. Through mutual respect, understanding, and collaboration, we can navigate the complexities of aging and fulfillment with grace and wisdom.

Here's what I'd like to tell the younger generation:

Plan for Yourself:

You are the most influential force shaping your life. You determine your happiness, emotional well-being, and responses to failure. Your actions can lead to success or be perceived as successful. Therefore, prioritize yourself first.

Be a Respectable Citizen:

Doing good aligns with the universe's positive energy and benefits the Earth. Environmental stewardship not only impacts neighbors but also cultivates a habit of citizenship that benefits everyone, especially future generations.

Earn a Living:

Dependency breeds contempt. While it may seem natural to desire financial support, earning a living fosters independence, structure, and appreciation. It contributes to personal growth and positively influences those around you.

Stay Healthy:

Prioritize longevity and vitality. The unexpected challenges like pandemics underscore the importance of maintaining good health. As health directly impacts wealth, strive to live as healthily as possible for as long as possible.

Save Early:

Establish a habit of saving in various aspects of life, from finances to relationships and environmental conservation. Early saving leads to long-term benefits, enhancing enjoyment and appreciation in the future.

Call Home:

Foster connections with loved ones by reaching out

regularly. Reap the rewards of communication by initiating contact and nurturing relationships with family members.

Dream On:

Embrace the power of dreaming and innovation. Millennials' penchant for dreaming fosters creativity and drives progress. Appreciate and encourage the next generation's innovative spirit.

Reinvent Yourself:

Continuously evolve and reinvent yourself. Embrace change and find new ways to add value to yourself and others. Transform old ideas into fresh perspectives and opportunities.

Have Fun:

Enjoy the journey of life. Find joy in every moment and prioritize activities that bring happiness and fulfillment.

Be Diverse:

Build relationships with people from diverse backgrounds, ages, and social statuses. Embrace diversity and learn from different perspectives to shape a more inclusive and equitable future.

You and your generation hold the power to shape the future. Embrace these principles to make a positive impact on the world and leave a lasting legacy of progress and prosperity.

From an idealistic view at 22 to reality at 62

At 22, I was just starting my family with one child and had recently married my wife, Han. I wonder whether reaching 62 felt like one of my greatest achievements or if it came unexpectedly.

At 22, I couldn't even anticipate what it would be like to be 62. My focus was on getting through each stage of raising a family—32, 42, and 52 were particularly daunting years as I navigated parenthood. I worried about providing for my children, guiding them to become responsible members of society rather than a burden. Daydreaming wasn't something I did much then. My vision for the future was simply to grow old surrounded by my family, offering wisdom to my grandchildren.

Comparing my idealistic view at 22 to reality at 62 is what gives my life purpose. I've come to understand that disappointment often stems from unfulfilled expectations. Over the years, I've had to adjust my expectations to fit the reality of my life at 62.

Today, I can speak with confidence because I've lived through the consequences of youth. With maturity and experience, I can articulate my thoughts and handle the outcomes. In my younger years, I lacked the ability to express my experiences fully because I hadn't yet accumulated enough wisdom. However, with each passing decade, I gained confidence in my ability to share my insights and give back to others… and along the way gathered a lot of real-life perspective to navigate life dearly.

How I addressed burnout

I was busy working to provide through my 20s and 30s, returning to college at 45 to earn a degree in Business Management. I call that 'burnout'. When you're pushing it, when you're struggling, when you're hustling, trying to make ends meet and keep things going, you don't see an exit strategy. But I knew I needed one. Getting old means you have to have a plan. You have to have enough money to fund yourself. You have to have something to do to occupy your time and so on. I just didn't see all of those things I was going to do, and since I was not even close to ending my work life or the career to put all of that together, I just knew that what I was doing was going to continue to burn me out. I needed to change what I'm doing. So, midstream, when that mental plan to go back to school was made, I took action, knowing all too well that I couldn't wait until I got old to fix things. You must fix things when you are young so that when you get older it's fixed. If you wait until you get old to fix it, it's too late. You may not have the energy nor the time. So the whole concept of growing old is to prepare as much in advance as possible.

Me-ism - Now I do all that scares me

When we spend all of those years of our lives in the 20s, 30s, 40s, and sometimes even into the 50s, depending on how early or late we start, we're 'giving' a lot of time, attention, and energy towards the building up of others [read family]. I got married at 19 and that did not give me any time to deal with me. Around those times, I didn't even know who I was, who I wanted to be, or who I could have been. Going through all those years, and by the time my younger son was 15 years old, I was burnt out... because I think I already took care of a lot of things - traveled to many nations, built so many houses, furnished them with the best of things, set up music equipment, bought vehicles for the older son, and so on... I was giving back to my household, giving back to my children, giving back to my employer, giving back to the community and society.

This book *The Art of Growing Old* talks a lot about me, and people like me, in the 60s and going beyond, to give back to self. I want to insist that it's OK to be selfish. It is OK to be selfish and concentrate on giving back to yourself. I want to assure all of you in my age group that you did a really good job of giving back to others, giving back to your family, and giving back to your employer and community. But understand that this also means we have emptied ourselves out. So, it is important that we fill ourselves back up – and that is giving back to yourself.

At this phase, I prefer a quality life that I can enjoy. Imagine going scuba diving, experiencing succession, and teaching and training in my industry at my own pace, by my own decisions, and with my own willpower. I am now doing things that used to scare the heck out of me, like learning how to manage firearms. The moment you slow down the more you become like molasses. Everything will coagulate, everything will get stiff and hard. I have convinced myself that I have to keep moving. I have to keep my brain moving and keep thinking. As I get older, I have to keep learning things as I experience them, and teach the things I've experienced.

Some people never made it to a university degree, and they say they want to do that, or they never got their masters. Go ahead! You can do it. I wanted to scuba dive, and I did. I wanted to experience going fast and far and I did that. Post-retirement, I took my motorcycle up to 175mph! I wouldn't do that again. But I wanted to taste it once, and I didn't hold myself back. I took class to learn how to do it all over again after being off a bike for 20 years and still looking for other machinery parts to put together or something so my hands and my brain keep working. All of these things are not really helping anyone else other than me, so that kind of 'me-ism' is selfish at this age. I don't believe in selfishness from another perspective. I don't believe in it because you shouldn't be selfish if you don't take care of all the things you're supposed to take care of. But you should be selfish and take care of yourself when you don't have those things, or even a younger person who does not have those responsibilities should be taking good care of themselves. When they have the responsibility, they should take care of that first. Then, when you don't have it again, like in this case when your kid has passed a certain age, you don't have the same responsibility to raise a kid. Then it's okay for people to be selfish and fill themselves up.

Sitting down and doing nothing is a resignation to die off faster than those who decide to pursue certain activities. When you look at the demographics of age, it's not necessarily about people who give up; it's about people who are actively engaged. Those who are still dancing, singing, writing music, drafting, engineering, trying, and failing—because failing is a significant part of learning. Keep in mind the risks of doing things, try new things, and always strive. It may not be at the same level as when you were 22 or 32, due to changes in body strength. But who is stopping you? If you want to climb that mountain, climb it a little slower. If you want to run that marathon, run it and take your time. If you want to swim in the ocean, scuba dive, see fish, or smell roses, do it at your own pace. There's no need to rush.

Since we're running out of time, we have to use our time wisely. It, indeed, is important for our age. If you want to exercise, do some exercise that makes you feel really good about yourself - your mental self, emotional self. Get medicated if you need, but enjoy to please yourself so you can help others because you helped yourself.

I always say a firefighter can't rescue people if he can't rescue himself. A lifeguard can't save a swimmer if they can't swim themselves. Although I want to give back a lot, I can't continue giving back if I don't fill myself up. Because by the time you're 50, 60, and beyond, you could be quite empty. You have to fill yourself up so that in your 70s and 80s, you can continue giving back—or doing something else; who knows?

The Art of Growing Old

My end-of-life strategy... applaud myself

Some people think older teachers are really wise. The wise person is the one who stays one page ahead of the student. It doesn't mean they have to know the whole thing in the book but every time you stay one page ahead of the student, it means what you learned yesterday, you can teach today. Some people think it's like a scientific approach, but it's not.

It's the moment we stop learning that we die. People should always embrace this principle. It's like the main rule of scuba diving: the moment you stop breathing, you're willing to die. You have to keep breathing. Life is like that, especially as you get older, you have to keep learning. It doesn't mean you have to go to school for more academics, but the school of real life is still there, and there's always something to learn. When I was invited as a guest of honor at the Academy in

Dubai on their graduation day, I stressed one key fact: "Go into things to see what you can learn. Don't go in to see what you can earn. By focusing on earnings, you may lose or spend them, and you'll always need to earn again and again. But when you focus on learning, you gain knowledge that lasts. You'll always seek to learn more, and never repeat the same lesson if you learn properly. And then you'll see how the earnings will follow."

I have been called back by the company I worked for. I enjoy every moment. Coming out to do teachings and training and document making and so on means I must have done something good because people don't call you back if you didn't do so well. This will be my 3rd time being called back by my former company. I am reminded of the old song, *'somewhere in my youth or childhood, I must have done something good.'* And I know they say get off the stage while the applause is still going, well sometimes I get to the point where I would applaud my damn self. I'm not waiting for anyone to applaud me anymore.

The difference between fighting for one's own goals or just letting it happen is a very fine line. That's the beauty of the art of growing old. As you grow older you can visualize that line and cross over it and cross back whenever you want. But when you're younger you almost have to let it flow. For instance, people worry so much about losing or quitting their jobs. In the past, it was very risky to quit a job. I try to tell people that jobs can hinder their creativity and dampen their entrepreneurial spirit. Yet, if you're not sure you can take the risk, it's okay to keep your job. However, if you're willing to take the risk and your circumstances are conducive, you should go for it. It's about letting things flow naturally rather than trying to manipulate them as if we have control over the universe.

We just have to sometimes go with it and see what happens. See where the cards fall. It's like flying through an asteroid belt when you hit that rock - it's either rock top or rock bottom. What happens in between is the nice part. The rock on top they call a 'glass ceiling' and the bottom they call 'rock bottom', but they're both the same. Sometimes we have to let it flow because we have very little control over any of it.

I made a lot of plans and did a lot of calculating. I calculated my entire end-of-life strategy up to the year 2050 in a spreadsheet, focusing on numerical and financial aspects.

We often think it takes money to get from point A to point B, but even without money, you might still have a place to live or food to eat. So, all those well-laid plans may go out the window, right? But making plans is good because it ensures you are always prepared. My good friend Greg Doakes says, "There's no such thing as being lucky. Luck is preparation." He is right because since our 20s, 30s, and 40s, leading into our 50s, we've been preparing for what we're going to encounter in our 50s, 60s, and 70s. Luck comes from preparation for a moment.

So, right now, as I've gotten older, I feel I'm in a place where I've been preparing for moments like this, and that's why I've been so 'lucky.' Luck is the accumulation of preparation, and you establish yourself for anything that comes your way. This has been true for me. I didn't know what would come my way, but I was prepared for it. That's another aspect of aging.

At 62, I am at a pleasant age. As Mr. B, I've been wanting to discuss the art of aging and what it entails. There's no manual for this, nor for life's various aspects. It's about taking risks, yet it's gratifying to share these experiences in a book, especially during moments of epiphany. Many reaching this age lack a concrete plan, similar to leaving a job and its accompanying community. It prompts introspection: Do I value myself? If I feel unneeded, do I need myself? It's nonsensical to wallow; instead, I hope to inspire action by sharing my journey.

Mr. B wasn't just an oil worker; he evolved into a public speaker, author, and giver. It's about spreading positive messages and fostering personal growth without financial burden. As I continue, I'll ensure I practice what I preach, from smiling to opening doors of opportunity. I intend to savor this phase, uncertain of how or when it'll end, but determined to make the most of it by giving back to myself.

The Art of Growing Old

10 tips to nurture connection across generations

There is the norm that we tend to segregate the old from the young in a lot of aspects. No one is to be blamed. As societal norms shift and technological advancements reshape the way we interact, the segregation between different age groups has become increasingly apparent. However, amidst these changes, the fundamental needs and desires of individuals across generations remain strikingly similar. Generation X, Millennials, and Gen Z may approach life with distinct perspectives and preferences, but at their core, they share a common longing for connection, purpose, and fulfillment.

Generation X, born between the early 1960s and late 1970s, grew up amidst economic and cultural upheaval, shaping their worldview with a blend of pragmatism and resilience.

Millennials, born between the early 1980s and mid-1990s, entered adulthood during a time of rapid technological advancement and globalization, fostering a desire for authenticity and social change. Gen Z, born from the mid-1990s to the early 2010s, are digital natives who prioritize inclusivity, diversity, and sustainability in their pursuits.

Despite these generational nuances, the basic necessities of life—such as shelter, education, mentorship, and community—remain constant. However, the circumstances and dynamics of modern society have inadvertently led to the segregation of age groups, hindering the opportunities for meaningful intergenerational connections. As individuals gravitate towards like-minded peers and digital echo chambers, the invaluable exchange of wisdom, experiences, and perspectives across generations is often overlooked.

Recognizing the inherent value in bridging the gap between generations, it is imperative for communities to prioritize intergenerational harmony and cooperation. By fostering mutual understanding, shared experiences, and collaborative efforts, communities can harness the richness of diverse perspectives and collective wisdom to address complex challenges and create a more inclusive and cohesive society.

Here are my 10 essential suggestions to promote joyful coexistence and graceful aging through intergenerational harmony.

By embracing these principles, communities can cultivate environments where individuals of all ages thrive together, contributing their unique talents and perspectives towards a common goal of collective well-being...

Intergenerational Housing Initiatives:

Encouraging communities where young and old thrive together. Propose housing designs that facilitate interaction between generations. Highlight the benefits of shared living arrangements for both older individuals and young families. Emphasize the importance of leveraging the knowledge and experience of older adults to enrich the lives of younger generations.

Revolutionizing Education and Workplace Dynamics:

Breaking down barriers to intergenerational learning. Advocate for programs that enable older adults to share their expertise with younger individuals in educational and workplace settings. Address concerns related to insurance and liability that hinder intergenerational collaboration. Suggest the implementation of initiatives like the 'bridges program' to bridge the gap between retiring employees and the next generation of workers.

Preserving and Passing on Wisdom:

Recognizing the value of intergenerational mentorship. Highlight the societal loss when valuable knowledge and experience are not passed down from older to younger generations. Propose mentorship programs that facilitate the transfer of wisdom and life lessons. Emphasize the role of older adults in guiding and supporting younger individuals through life's challenges.

Creating Spaces for Intergenerational Dialogue:

Rediscovering the lost art of sharing stories and wisdom. Advocate for the revival of traditional practices, such as storytelling and communal gatherings, to facilitate intergenerational communication. Highlight the benefits of meaningful conversations and shared experiences between generations. Encourage the creation of inclusive spaces where individuals of all ages can come together to learn from one another.

Promoting Intergenerational Technology Literacy:

Empowering seniors and younger generations alike with digital skills. Advocate for programs that bridge the digital divide between older adults and younger individuals, providing training and support in using technology effectively. Highlight the importance of intergenerational collaboration in navigating the digital landscape and staying connected in an increasingly digital world. Encourage initiatives that facilitate knowledge sharing and mentorship in areas such as online communication, digital literacy, and cybersecurity, fostering intergenerational learning and mutual empowerment.

Embracing the Art of Growing Old:

Finding fulfillment in giving back and sharing experiences. Emphasize the importance of older adults embracing their role as mentors and contributors to society. Encourage a shift in mindset towards aging as an opportunity to give back and share wisdom. Highlight the mutual benefits of intergenerational relationships in fostering personal growth and fulfillment.

Promoting Intergenerational Volunteerism:

Engaging seniors in meaningful community service.

Encourage older adults to participate in volunteer activities that benefit the community and provide opportunities for intergenerational interaction. Highlight the positive impact of seniors' contributions to community service and the valuable lessons they can impart to younger volunteers. Advocate for the creation of volunteer programs that specifically focus on bridging the generation gap and fostering connections between seniors and youth.

Supporting Intergenerational Wellness Programs:

Promoting health and well-being across age groups. Propose the development of wellness programs that cater to the needs of both older adults and younger individuals, fostering a sense of community and mutual support. Highlight the benefits of intergenerational fitness classes, recreational activities, and wellness workshops in promoting physical, mental, and emotional well-being. Encourage partnerships between senior centers, schools, and community organizations to create inclusive wellness programs that cater to individuals of all ages.

Fostering Intergenerational Entrepreneurship:

Encouraging collaboration and innovation across generations. Promote initiatives that encourage collaboration between older adults with entrepreneurial experience and younger individuals with fresh ideas and technological skills. Highlight the benefits of intergenerational entrepreneurship in fostering innovation, creating new business opportunities, and addressing societal challenges. Advocate for networking events, and incubator spaces that facilitate collaboration and knowledge sharing between generations in the business world.

Celebrating Intergenerational Diversity:

Embracing cultural exchange and understanding across age groups. Encourage intergenerational initiatives that celebrate cultural diversity and promote cross-cultural understanding and appreciation. Highlight the importance of intergenerational dialogue in breaking down stereotypes, bridging cultural divides, and fostering a sense of unity and belonging. Advocate for cultural exchange programs, intergenerational festivals, and multicultural events that bring together individuals of all ages to celebrate diversity and promote intergenerational harmony.

MINDFUL MUSINGS

Reflect on a significant decision you made that truly aligned with your personal values and desires. How did living on your own terms impact your happiness and fulfillment?

_____

_____

_____

_____

What societal pressures or expectations have you had to navigate to stay true to yourself? How did you overcome them?

_____

_____

List three pieces of advice you would give to someone younger. How have these truths guided your own life decisions?

Think about a time when you didn't follow conventional wisdom. What was the outcome, and what did you learn from that experience?

Compare your dreams and goals at age 22 with your current reality. What have you achieved, and what has changed over time?

Reflect on an idealistic belief you held in your youth. How has your perspective shifted as you've aged?

_____

_____

_____

_____

How do you want to be remembered by your loved ones? What legacy do you hope to leave behind?

_____

_____

_____

_____

Think about your biggest accomplishments. How can you celebrate these achievements and use them to shape your end-of-life strategy?

What actions can you take to strengthen your relationships with people from different generations? Reflect on the benefits of these connections.

_____

_____

_____

Describe a meaningful intergenerational relationship in your life. What have you learned from this person, and how has it enriched your life?

_____

_____

_____

_____

_____

How has your perception of aging changed over the years? What positive aspects do you see in growing older?

What intergenerational relationships have had the most impact on your life? How have they influenced your perspective on aging?

Reflect on a recent experience where curiosity led you to learn something new. How did this experience enhance your life?

_____

_____

_____

_____

_____

Describe a significant change or challenge you've faced recently. How did you manage to adapt and thrive despite the difficulties?

_____

_____

_____

What strategies have you used to embrace change throughout your life? How can you apply these strategies to future transitions?

How have conversations with younger or older generations shaped your understanding of life and aging? Share an example of a particularly impactful interaction.

Reflect on the importance of self-compassion. How can being kind to yourself help you navigate the challenges of aging with grace and resilience?

The Art of Growing Old

SECTION: V

Silver Seniors – The Art of Thriving Beyond Retirement

As we age, we don't lose youth we take from it

Being emotionally empowered and cultivating a culture of fun is the way to live in one's senior years,

- Sandi

The Art of Growing Old

Sandi Rich Saksena Rocking at 72

The Art of Growing Old

I give no permission to categorize me, label me! For me, life as 'me' began at age 44!

I started my married life in Kuwait – a happy wife, happy mommy, immersed in my family. My husband's prospects improved by leaps and bounds; we were truly living an amazing life. We come from middle-class families that lived a good life on carefully planned budgets. However, soon the budget lifestyle gave way to splurge style, and for 20 years it was an easy street! My kids grew up during this phase - 5 star all the way… homes, schools, vacations, travel… luxury living!

Dreams descended to nightmares as I set foot in Dubai. I was so immersed in my role as the supportive dutiful wife I never questioned the move to Dubai, feeling secure in the knowledge that we would continue our journey onwards and upwards. The decision, the timing, impact, the repercussions, consequences, nothing was discussed, I just accepted. The contract my husband had signed fell through and with it our lives were thrown into turmoil.

Dreadfulness, anger, frustration, confusion, resentment, misery, words are not enough to express the feelings we were experiencing. No income to cover rent, groceries, school/college fees. My spouse was suffering from insomnia, stress, and fatigue. He collapsed at a meeting. I rushed to the government hospital and broke down when I saw him lying in the general ward. This was a man who had the top-of-the-line medical insurance, who had always been treated in the best hospitals with no expenses spared. Yet here he lay in a general ward because we had no money, no insurance. I felt emotionally and psychologically shattered, my sense of security crumbling, leaving me feeling helpless in a precarious world. Confusion, fear, panic, and more overwhelmed me. The need of the hour was for me to get a job. However, I couldn't write a CV. Despite being a college graduate, at 44 years old, I was computer illiterate and had no work experience.

I faced bitter rejections and taunts… from 'no experience? Are you for real?'; 'Lady at your age seriously? You gotta have more than dress well, speak well!' Dismissed by supercilious HR managers and having exhausted all my friendly connections, my tenacity and belief in myself strengthened. I wasn't going to surrender to circumstances, and no one was going to dictate what I could and would do except me.

I cultivated absolute belief and set a clear intent. I told myself, 'You are always in-charge of you even though social conditioning wants you to believe otherwise'.

Eventually, I was offered the job of a financial planning consultant. I was elated, but when I heard I would get NO salary, only commission, I crumbled within. I was looking for a fixed income. In that state of mind I could not and did not see the potential for unlimited income. I was so clouded by fear and panic.

Selling life insurance in the UAE in the 90s was a challenge! All I had was attitude, belief, courage/charisma, determination, and loads of energy. I threw all qualms to the winds and began knocking on doors cold calling, made countless phone calls and joined networking groups. No matter how many rejections, I never lost faith. Gradually, I developed confidence and my income grew. The lessons I learned then keep me in good stead even today.

In 2000, a near-death experience on the operating table gave me a new lease on life. I found myself on the path of self-discovery… I rose from the immersion of 'self for others' to 'me for me'. I rediscovered my true self and I have been in the driver's seat, since.

I find it so motivating and empowering to be able to decide for myself what I want to do. I upgraded myself in different areas of life. My income grew, so did my knowledge, personal and professional development. I discovered facets of me that excited and energized me. I studied, got certified and qualified for international conventions, so much so today I'm invited to speak in different countries.

Skydiving, zip lining, white water rafting level +5 mushing with the huskies in the Arctic circle, pilgrimages to Mount Kailash x2 walking at 18,500 feet, I continue to seek out physical and mental challenges. I have even visited Macchu Picchu in Peru and done the Ayahuasca twice.

Life experiences are one's best teacher and what it has taught me is that all the answers and solutions lie within us. I am tuned into my internal GPS - my intuition, inner voice, my soul! I am currently preparing for the Dubai Run, where I'll be running a 10k route this November.

Today age 72, I have my work, my seminars, my writing, my speaking engagements, podcasts, fitness challenges and to add walking on the ramp as a model. I am emotionally empowered.

Being 'serious' doesn't get it done. Things get done when you are having fun. Smile and you have begun. Enjoy what you do and you have won. I call this the 'Culture of fun'!

Staying active and engaged post-retirement is key to health and happiness

- Ahmad Al Awadhi

Ahmad Al Awadhi Rukni is an Art Ambassador at 65

The Art of Growing Old

The Art of Growing Old

I am a school dropout who started working at age 14!

Today, at 65, I find contentment in the life I've lived. My father owned two shops in Sharjah before the UAE was founded. At 14, I began helping him in our general store, which stocked everything from shoes to electronics, toys, and household items. After four months, my father's partnership with my uncle ended, and my uncle failed to honor his promise of paying me Dh100 a month. My father stepped in to ensure I received my salary. Thus, in 1969, I earned Dh400, a substantial amount at the time.

Initially, my parents urged me to return to school, but I found my calling in managing the shop. Selling towels to British soldiers not only helped me financially but also taught me spoken English, a skill not offered in school then. As my proficiency in managing the shop grew, my parents ceased urging me to return to school. At 15, my father rewarded my dedication by giving me a 25% stake in the shops and appointing me as the cashier. Over the next decade, I worked alongside my father and four brothers, expanding our business to Dubai.

However, differences with my older brother led me to part

ways after a decade. While I aimed to save, he spent lavishly, including on a Mercedes car and a villa. Despite my father's attempts to mediate, my brother refused to relinquish control of assets. Determined to make my own way, I declined further assistance from my father and struck out on my own at 25.

My first independent venture, a small shop, failed. Instead of seeking help from my father, I started an optical shop in Sharjah with a partner, which succeeded, and I expanded to Dubai. Gradually, I ventured into the food industry with a 'Subway' franchise. Although plans to expand didn't materialize, I still own one outlet in Deira City Centre. Later, I acquired the 'New York Fries' franchise across the UAE, which I continue to hold.

Alongside my business ventures, I delved into the share market, purchasing shares from banks and investing in properties, including land in Sharjah. I also collaborated with an Iranian associate in Sharjah, buying scrap ships from Singapore, repairing them in Ajman, and reselling them for significant profits. However, my trust was betrayed when he cheated me out of Dh1.5 million and left for Canada. Part of the money belonged to my friends, but I repaid each one of them within a couple of months and refocused on my optical business.

Meanwhile, there was growing pressure at home for me to get married, but I was determined to have my own home first. Although my mother insisted that my father buy me a house, I wanted to achieve it independently. With Dh80,000 in savings, I took a loan of Dh50,000 and purchased a 3-bedroom villa for Dh120,000. My father was initially surprised by my decision to seek a loan, but I wanted to do it on my own. I rented out the villa for Dh12,000 per month and paid off the loan. After a year, I completely refurbished it. Then, I got married and moved into the villa with my wife. Eighteen years later, as my family grew, I bought a larger villa.

Although I have good business acumen, I am an artist at heart. From my early school days, I sketched on any scrap of paper I could find. Without formal training, I pursued art independently, experimenting with watercolors and gradually mastering the techniques over time. Most of my old sketches are lost, but painting became my refuge—a way to destress and express myself. I typically begin painting after my family retires at around 10 PM, playing classical music and painting until 4 AM. One night, I was so immersed in my work that I mistook the rising sun for a spotlight. Painting has now become a routine for me!

Today, I spend more time with the art community, attending events and supporting fellow artists. My involvement extends internationally, with exhibitions in various countries, including Korea, India, and Georgia. I love artists; they are sensitive and humble people. Over the years, I have changed. I smile a lot now. I consider myself a successful man because I am happy and content today. Success in my youth was different; it was about making money. Now, success means indulging in my art, gardening, and ensuring my wife and children are happy. My thoughts are more about my children's future.

For those approaching retirement, I suggest remaining active. Staying at home can lead to stagnation. Whether through business pursuits or social interactions, staying engaged is essential for maintaining health and happiness in later years. Starting something new may seem daunting, but our wealth of experience is invaluable.

Though I am less visible in the day-to-day operations of my business now, I still guide and manage my team. While I may not have the same level of recognition as before, I find fulfillment in being known more for my artistic endeavors than my business ventures. I have no regrets.

Looking back, I feel I could have graduated, as educated Emiratis were few back then, and those with a college degree were employed by the government. Perhaps I could have become an ambassador. But I am not sad about it. I am recognized today for my art wherever I go.

To live a fulfilling post-retirement life, one must maintain health, nurture relationships and ensure financial freedom

- Anjini Laitu

Anjini Laitu aims to be world's top abstract painter at 83

The Art of Growing Old

The Art of Growing Old

At 64 years of age, I went to college to study art!

I always harbored a deep desire to pursue art, but practicalities and responsibilities kept me from it during my younger years. My parents insisted I take up technical education so I can earn a living. So, after completing my education, I joined the Thapar Group, a leading textile and paper company in India. I spent 37 years working in various capacities within the group until I retired at the age of 55.

In 1995, shortly before retiring, our company received an offer from the UAE to assist in setting up a glass bottle plant. My son was doing his MBA and I didn't want to disturb his studies by relocating him. Also, I didn't know driving. Despite my initial reluctance I eventually agreed because the rewards were substantial. I joined a team of 150 other people from different Thapar groups to establish the company – Al Tajir Glass Factory in Dubai. I served as the commercial manager for about 6 years, before I finally retired.

Retirement provided me with the opportunity to explore my passion. In 2004, at the age of 64, I enrolled in the Sharjah Art Institute to study painting. Though I initially pursued the course to obtain a degree rather than to learn, I soon realized that my childhood experience in textile painting was invaluable.

Even before formal training, I had dabbled in fabric painting, which I continued as a part-time endeavor while working in India. Using unconventional materials like thick cloth coated with local gum and using turmeric powder and coal dust, I created unique artworks that have since become some of my most prized possessions.

My journey as an artist gained momentum when I hosted my first exhibition at the Arab Cultural Club in Sharjah, garnering attention from Sharjah TV and Arabic magazines. Subsequent exhibitions, including one showcasing tile paintings, further solidified my presence in the art community. Participating in events like World Art Dubai for seven consecutive years allowed me to showcase my work and gain recognition.

Maintaining a sense of purpose as I grow older is quite simple for me - I just want to paint. I've left behind my earlier life and if someone were to ask me about my previous work in paper making, I wouldn't be able to provide an answer.

However, I need to stress one point here. Financial freedom, especially in senior years, is crucial. It's important to have the means to indulge in passions without the pressure of earning from them. For me, financial freedom means being capable of funding my activities for at least the next 20 years after retirement. Initially, I received help from my wife and son, but ultimately, it's essential to either support oneself or have support from family members.

So, if you ask me what I consider is important in post-retirement life. It is family, health and financial freedom. Family holds immense importance to me. Without their support, nothing would be possible. Currently, I live with my wife, son, daughter-in-law, grandson, and a house help. That is also success for me.

In fact, the definition of success has evolved in meaning for me over the years. In my youth, it meant reaching the top management position in my career. In my 50s, success shifted to ensuring my family's happiness and fulfillment of their goals. Now, success is not about money but about the love of people and maintaining meaningful relationships.

For those without hobbies post-retirement, I suggest finding something that brings joy and fulfillment. Engaging in social activities or volunteering can be equally satisfying. Also, pay attention to your health. I gave up on red meat and smoking on the advice of my doctor. Also, I eat very little now. And I feel healthy. I keep physically active by doing my own work. I don't ask for a glass of water; I get up and take it myself. I make my own canvas. I do basic yoga a couple of times a week.

Painting every day keeps me happy, and I maintain a structured daily routine. I paint every night from about 11 PM until 3 AM. I wake up by 11 AM, have a light breakfast of tea and biscuits, and then paint for an hour. When my wife returns from the salon, we have a late lunch around 3:30 PM. Afterward, I take a two-hour nap. By the time I wake up, my son and his family have returned from work. Then, it's family time until they go to bed, after which I pick up my paintbrush again.

My advice to retirees and the young alike is to cultivate a hobby and save early for old age. Happiness and health go hand in hand, but financial stability is equally important for a fulfilling life.

At 83, my dream is to become the top abstract painter in the world, known for my unique style. While I've received numerous local awards and recognition, achieving this dream would be the pinnacle of my artistic journey.

I have absolutely no regrets. God has been kind. I have lived a contented life. To live a fulfilling life in old age it is important you have a passion or hobby, maintain good health, nurture relationships and ensuring financial stability.

The Art of Growing Old

The math of aging stops at giving back to self

Our only real companion, as we walk this planet, is time! Have you given this a thought?

Can we really embrace time, in the real sense of the word? The answer is both 'Yes' and 'No'. Time is an illusion. We cannot feel it, see it or touch it and yet we know it. There was time before we were born and there will be time after we are gone. In between our entry and exit, time' walks beside us.

How do we treat 'time' and allow it to treat us? Do we honor it? Do we ridicule it? Are we afraid of it? Do we embrace it?...A Casio watch on our wrist will show us 'the time'. But a Patek Philippe on our wrist will show us 'our time'!

In other words, it's how we treat time that makes time define our existence. So, let's make it worthwhile!

As I wrote in the beginning of this book, our first year represents 100 percent of our life. In year 10, one year represents 10 percent of our life lived, and so on. Each annual journey accounts for a mere 10 percent of our life's narrative. Imagine the shrinkage of percentage as we reach the milestone of 50 years – by then, each passing year constitutes a mere two percent of our storied existence.

This exponential shrinkage in significance might be the elusive culprit behind the illusion that time accelerates with each passing year. Yet, amidst this perceived hastening, we acknowledge the unchanging rhythm of sixty seconds in a minute, sixty minutes in an hour, and the completion of 365 days in a year. Day by day, we chug along, calling it one day at a time and fulfilling a sense of purpose as we age.

Time is both a tangible measure and an elusive illusion. As children, a year felt like an eternity, a boundless stretch of time filled with possibilities. As we age, each year seems to slip through our fingers more quickly than the last. This perception is a testament to the psychological phenomenon where each passing year becomes a smaller fraction of our lived experience. The constancy of time remains, but our perception warps its flow.

To reconcile this dual nature of time, we must acknowledge its relentless march while also embracing the illusion it creates. Time, in its unyielding precision, offers us the framework within which we live our lives. Yet, it is the quality of our experiences, not the quantity of years, which defines our journey.

Honoring Time Through Giving Back to Self:

Ultimately, the most effective way to honor time is by giving back to ourselves. This isn't about selfishness; it's about self-care and self-compassion. By nurturing our physical, mental, and emotional well-being, we ensure that we have the strength and clarity to pursue our purpose and passions.

This is the art of growing old with grace, wisdom, and fulfillment. Self-care involves:

Physical Health:

Maintaining a healthy lifestyle through regular exercise, a balanced diet, and adequate rest.

Mental Health:

Engaging in activities that stimulate our minds, seeking help when needed, and practicing stress management techniques.

Emotional Health:

Building strong relationships, expressing our feelings, and practicing self-compassion.

Financial Health:

Being prudent in saving enough funds so we do not depend on others for our basic needs.

Living prudently and focusing on our unique journey ensures that we do not become disillusioned or demoralized by others' lives. When we compare ourselves to others, we risk losing sight of our own path and the progress we've made.
Time unfolds differently for each person, shaped by their experiences, aspirations, and values. By honoring our individual journey, we embrace the richness of our own story, free from the pressures of external expectations. This allows us to live authentically and find fulfillment in the present moment, rather than chasing an illusory standard of success.

In our partnership with time, we discover the power of acceptance and gratitude. We learn to cherish each moment, recognizing its inherent value regardless of external measures of achievement.

Through the highs and lows, we navigate life's twists and turns with resilience and grace, guided by the steady rhythm of time's passage. We find solace in the knowledge that our journey has been uniquely ours, shaped by the choices we've made and the experiences we've embraced.

In the art of growing old, we come to understand that time is not our adversary but our most trusted companion. It is the constant presence that accompanies us through life's joys and sorrows, offering us the opportunity to savor each moment and live with purpose. With gratitude in our hearts and wisdom in our souls, we embrace the journey ahead, knowing that our partnership with time is the greatest gift of all.

Take care of yourself dear reader,
Nurture your soul, love yourself
Pamper your heart, your body, your mind
Only thus will

The Art of Growing Old

True happiness fill you, and
Your essence linger on
In the sands of time

MINDFUL MUSINGS

How do you feel about the idea that time is your only real companion throughout life? Describe a moment when this felt particularly true or false.

_____

_____

_____

_____

_____

In what ways have you noticed the passage of time affecting your priorities and goals? Provide specific examples.

_____

_____

_____

Reflect on a time when you felt completely in sync with the passage of time. What were you doing, and how did it feel?

Conversely, think of a moment when you felt disconnected from time. What circumstances led to this feeling, and how did you cope?

_____

_____

_____

Describe a routine or habit that you have developed to make the most of your time. How has it improved your daily life?

_____

_____

_____

_____

Have you ever felt like you were wasting time? What activities or mindsets contributed to this feeling, and how did you address it?

_____

_____

_____

_____

_____

How do you balance the feeling of time speeding up with the reality that every minute and hour remains constant? What strategies help you stay present?

_____

_____

_____

_____

Write about an experience where your perception of time

significantly differed from the actual time passed. How did this impact your actions or decisions?

_____

_____

_____

_____

What activities bring you the most joy and fulfillment? How can you ensure you make time for these activities regularly?

_____

_____

_____

_____

Reflect on the importance of self-care in your life. How do you plan to prioritize self-care moving forward, especially as you age?

Think about the concept of nurturing your soul. What practices help you feel spiritually and emotionally nourished?

The Art of Growing Old

_____

_____

_____

How can you show love and compassion to yourself in ways that you might currently neglect? List specific actions you can take.

_____

_____

_____

_____

_____

The Art of Growing Old

Scuba diving is a sport I took up post-retirement. I cherished every moment I spent with my younger son Tim, as we trained together.

After giving the commencement speech to young adults in Dubai. My intent was to inspire youngsters embarking on the next phase of their lives.

With my business partner Krizzia Ann Loyang Tanabe. Doing business was a conscious choice I made post-retirement to ensure financial freedom in my senior years.

This poster humbles me, as much as it makes me proud. Being the brand ambassador in my 60s proves there's nothing we cannot do if we have our intentions right, our heart clear and be focused.

This is what I mean by enjoying the freedom retirement deserves! Reviving my love for riding now… It keeps me staying refreshed and feeling youthful.

Mentoring the future… Speaking to school children in the Philippines. I consider it my privilege to guide the next generation toward success and growth.

Bangladeshi butterflies are a bunch of talented, smart kids whom I never miss a chance to interact with. This is after I hosted a luncheon for them.

Motivating adults to reignite their passions and embrace new possibilities. No matter the stage in life, we all need a push to reach our full potential.

Balancing business with a touch of melody because entertainment fuels creativity and uplifts spirit.

Each time I take the stage, I grow as a speaker. Post-retirement, sharing my best experiences is my way of giving back – coming full circle to inspire others.

AUTHOR BIO

Bertrand Stephen St Louis, known as Mr. B, is an inspiring coach and the host of the podcast 'Free Talk With Mr. B.' Raised by a single mother, he started working at age 12. Determined to better himself and help others, he went back to college at 45 to earn a degree in Business Management.

After a successful 35-year career in the energy industry, Mr. B decided to follow his passion for helping people. He started 'Free Talk with Mr. B' to give ordinary people a platform to share their stories. His work has taken him to over 36 countries, and his podcast recently hit a milestone of 10,000 downloads.

Mr. B's first book, *The Art of Giving Back*, received rave reviews and has a global readership, reaching audiences in Nigeria, the Philippines, India, the US, and the UAE.

Mr. B enjoys dancing, cooking, and singing karaoke.

He is the brand ambassador for iFranchise and lives in the US with his wife, Han.

To learn more about Mr. B and his services, visit www.freetalkwithmrb.com

www.ingramcontent.com/pod-product-compliance
Lightning Source LLC
Chambersburg PA
CBHW042141010526
44113CB00031B/103